Harmony, Melody & Composition

PAUL STURMAN

Professor of Harmony and Composition
at the London College of Music

D1514375

CAMBRIDGE
UNIVERSITY PRESS

PUBLISHED BY THE PRESS SYNDICATE OF THE UNIVERSITY OF CAMBRIDGE
The Pitt Building, Trumpington Street, Cambridge, United Kingdom

CAMBRIDGE UNIVERSITY PRESS
The Edinburgh Building, Cambridge CB2 2RU, UK   www.cup.cam.ac.uk
40 West 20th Street, New York, NY 10011–4211, USA   www.cup.org
10 Stamford Road, Oakleigh, Melbourne 3166, Australia
Ruiz de Alarcón 13, 28014 Madrid, Spain

© Longman Group UK Limited 1983
© Cambridge University Press 1995

First published 1983 by Longman Group UK Limited
First published 1995 by Cambridge University Press
Reprinted 1997, 1999

Printed in the United Kingdom at the University Press, Cambridge

A catalogue record for this book is available from the British Library

Paperback: ISBN 0 521 56908 7

CONTENTS

Musical motion

One note heard on its own is not music. But as soon as this note moves to another note music is set in motion.

Musical motion can happen in a number of ways – in melody, harmony and rhythm. Some music consists only of rhythm but this is rare. Most music is a mixture of two or more types of motion.

Rhythmical motion

Rhythm is the oldest and most basic kind of musical motion. Before man could speak he showed his feelings by moving his body and by making rhythmical noises. In this example, rhythm is used to make musical motion without melody or harmony being used at all.

A regimental band drum solo rhythm

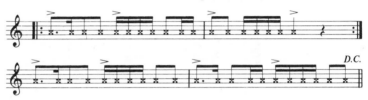

Melodic motion

The most simple melodic motion is the repetition of a single note. One-note melody is heard in some primitive music and also in religious chanting.

Plainchant: *Gloria*

Glo - ry be to the Fa-ther and to the Son

In the hands of a skilful composer one-note melodic repetition can sound really exciting.

Khachaturian: Sabre Dance from *Gayaneh*

An example of melody which uses two different notes is the cuckoo's call. Many composers have used this call in their music.

Daquin: *Le coucou*

(Cu - ckoo)

This two-note melody can quickly become tiring to the ear if heard
for any length of time. The more usual melodic motion occurs when
a note moves to the next above or below, then perhaps to one
higher still before returning to the original note.

Plainchant: *Amen*

Stepwise melodic motion often makes smooth and flowing music.

Brahms: Waltz in G, Op. 39 no. 10

Composers often use leaping motion to produce energetic and
exciting melodies.

Wagner: *The Ride of the Valkyries*

But there are not many melodies which are made up of just steps
or just leaps. Composers usually combine the two to give variety
and a good balance.

Dvořák: *Slavonic Dance* in G minor, Op. 46 no. 8

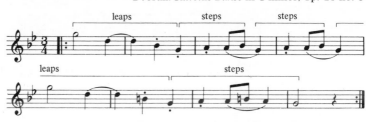

Range

Range is the distance between the highest and lowest note of a
piece of music.

Melodies with a small range (about 1–5 notes) often tend to be
calm and gentle in style.

Rakhmaninov: Piano Concerto no. 2 in C minor

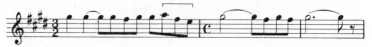

Melodies with a wide range (more than 10 notes) have a more open and bold quality. There is more room for the melody to spread out.

Walton: 'Popular Song' from *Façade Suite* no. 2

A large number of melodies use a medium range of notes (6–10 notes). This medium range is suitable for vocal music, as the range of the average voice is not as great as most instruments.

Rodgers and Hammerstein: 'Oh, what a beautiful mornin'' from *Oklahoma!*

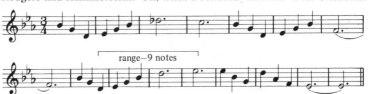

Even instrumental music by Classical and Romantic composers, such as Haydn, Mozart, Beethoven and Schubert, often uses a medium range of notes.

Mozart: Symphony no. 40 in G minor (1st movement)

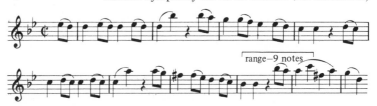

Harmonic motion

Harmonic motion is not so obvious as melodic or rhythmic motion. The melody is often on the surface of the music, but the harmony is underneath the surface. Even so, most people are aware of the harmony when listening to music. Harmonic motion is most noticeable in music with a slowly changing melody or rhythm. In this example the motion comes from the harmony rather than from the melody or rhythm. The chords seem to move the music along.

Bach: Chorale Prelude *Erbarm' dich mein*, BWV721

In music of the past few centuries, melody and harmony are closely related. In some music, melody is the more important; in other music it is the harmony which takes priority.

WORK ON MUSICAL MOTION AND RANGE

Play or sing through these melodies, then copy them into your manuscript books. Complete these exercises using the example as a guide.

1. Mark steps ⋰⋱ or leaps ⌐¬ between each two notes.
2. Does the melody move mainly by step, mainly in leaps, or by a mixture of steps and leaps?
3. What is the range – small, medium or wide?
4. Put a circle round the highest and lowest notes and join them together with a dotted line.
5. What is the total range of notes used?

Example: French-Canadian Folk Song: *Alouette*

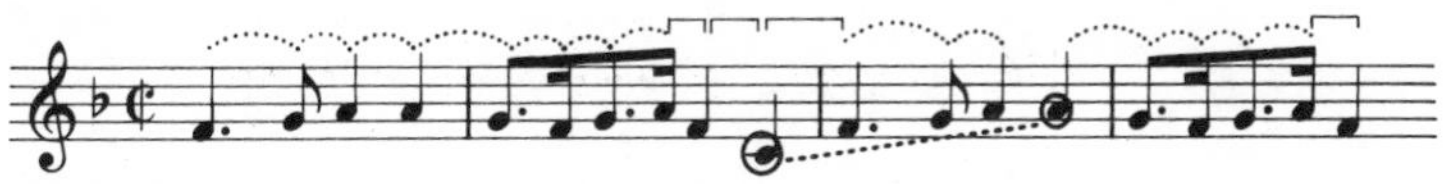

2. Mainly by step 3. Medium range 5. Range–6 notes

Mozart: *The Marriage of Figaro*

1. 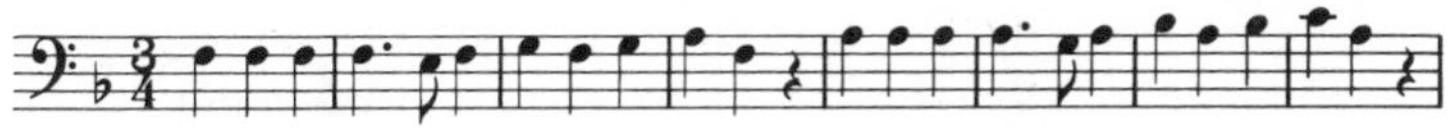

Dvořák: *Terzetto*, Op. 74

2. 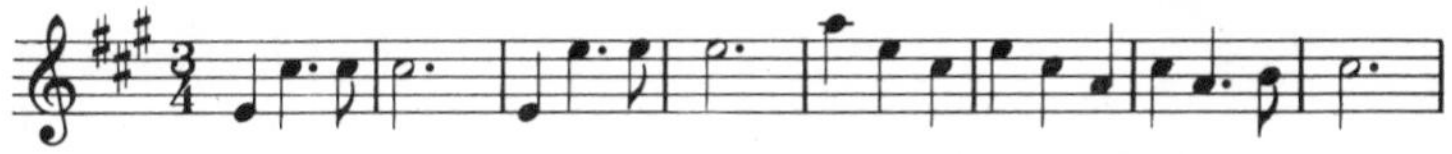

Mahler: Symphony no. 1 in D

3. 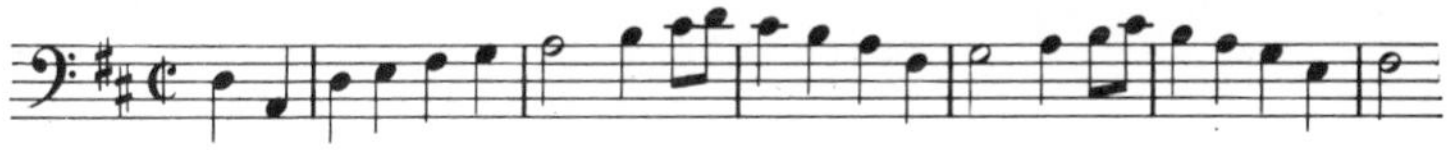

Folk Tune: *Country Gardens*

4. 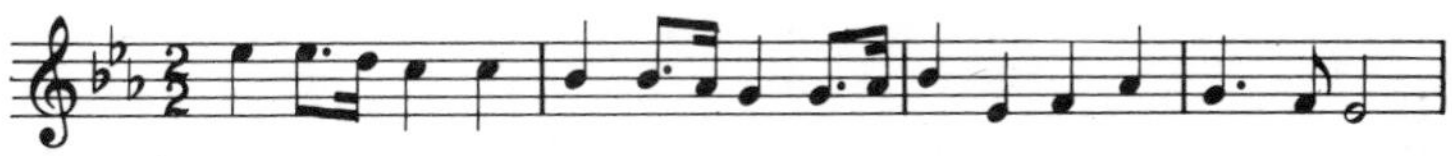

Chopin: Prelude in A, Op. 28 no. 7

5. 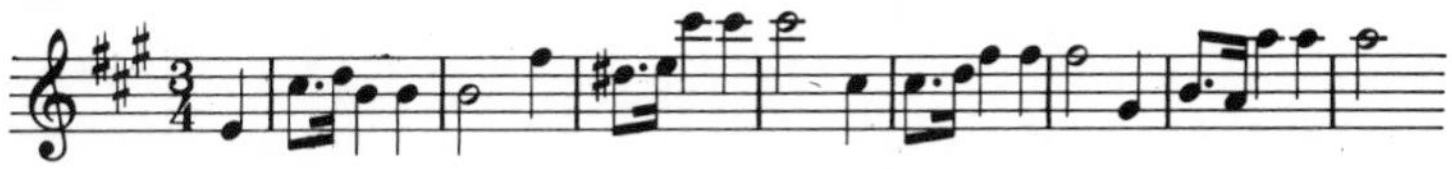

St Anthony Chorale

6. 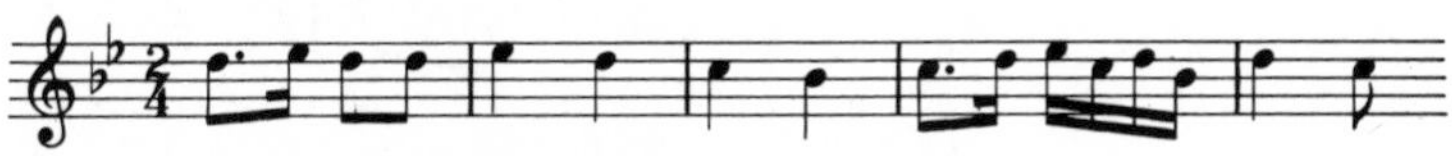

Intervals (1)

An interval is the exact distance between two notes. The simplest way to identify intervals is by using the eight notes of a major scale as a guide.

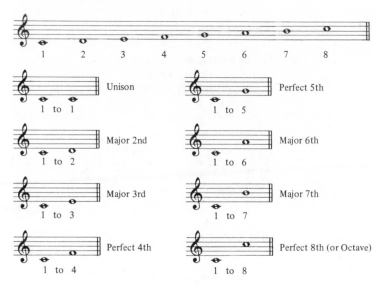

**Perfect
intervals**

You may wonder why the 4th, 5th and 8ve (octave) are called perfect and the others major. These names go back in time to the Middle Ages. The music of the early Christian church (called organum) used only the intervals of a 4th, 5th and 8ve. All other intervals were thought to sound harsh and were therefore unsuitable for church music. The 4th, 5th and 8ve were the only intervals which were 'perfect' for use at this time. Times have changed and we no longer think this way, but the label 'perfect' has stuck.

Here are some examples of intervals used by composers in their music.

Perfect 4th (P4)

Brahms: Symphony no. 1 (4th movement)

Perfect 5th (P5)

Dukas: *The Sorcerer's Apprentice*

Violins, violas and cellos all tune their strings in perfect 5ths.

Perfect 8ve (P8)

Dvořák: *Slavonic Dance*, Op. 46 no. 1

Intervals of a 2nd, 3rd, 6th and 7th

These intervals have two different forms – Major (M) and minor (m). A minor interval is smaller than a major interval by one semitone. The best way of understanding tones and semitones is to think of a piano keyboard.

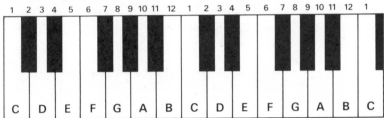

A semitone is the distance between two keys next to one another, either black or white, for example 1–2, 5–6, 7–8. A tone consists of two semitones, for example 1–3, 5–7, 8–10.

Here are some examples of pieces of music using major and minor intervals.

Major 2nd (M2)

Bach: *Two-Part Invention* no. 1 in C

Minor 2nd (m2)

Prokofiev: March of the Hunters from *Peter and the Wolf*

Major 3rd (M3)

Mozart: Piano Sonata in C minor, K457

Minor 3rd (m3)

Mozart: Piano Sonata in C minor, K457

Major 6th (M6)

My bonnie lies over the ocean

My bon - nie lies   o - ver the   o - cean

Minor 6th (m6)

Chopin: Waltz in C sharp minor, Op. 64 no. 2

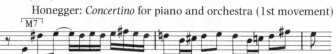

Major 7th (M7)

Honegger: *Concertino* for piano and orchestra (1st movement)

Minor 7th (m7)

Bernstein: 'Somewhere' from *West Side Story*

There's   a   place   for us,   Some-where a   place   for us

The musical examples above show intervals which rise.
Intervals can also fall. Here is just one example of major 2nds
and minor 2nds with a falling pattern.

Beethoven: Violin Sonata ('The Spring'), Op. 24

**Intervals
and their
personalities**

In all music, from early times to the present day, the use of
different kinds of interval has helped to give music its own
personality or character. In some cases one interval can influence
the character of a whole piece of music. Berg's Violin Concerto, for
example, is based on a series of major and minor 3rds.

These examples illustrate some of the characteristics of intervals,
but no interval is restricted to only one type of expression. Their
uses have changed throughout musical history.

It is important at this stage to know the difference between an
interval in melody (a melodic interval) and an interval in harmony
(an harmonic interval). A melodic interval is two notes, one
followed by another. An harmonic interval is two notes sounded
together.

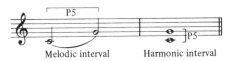

Melodic interval   Harmonic interval

Major and minor 2nds

A 2nd is the smallest interval. Music which moves by step (or in 2nds) is often smooth and flowing. It nearly always consists of major *and* minor 2nds.

Smetana: 'Vltava' from *Ma vlást* (*My Country*)

When only major 2nds are used, the melody is often misty rather than clear-cut. The French composer Debussy used a scale made up entirely of major 2nds (the whole-tone scale).

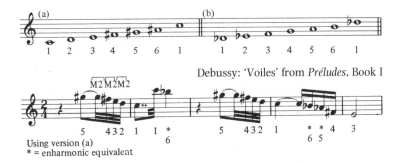

Debussy: 'Voiles' from *Préludes*, Book I

Using version (a)
* = enharmonic equivalent

A series of semitones (minor 2nds) is called *chromatic* movement. Its effect is often emotional and exciting.

Chopin: Etude in A minor, Op. 10 no. 2

Harmonic 2nds have a biting or pungent sound. The well-known tune *Chopsticks* starts with an harmonic major 2nd repeated six times.

Chopsticks

In this example trumpets produce an attacking effect with their clashing harmonic 2nds.

Rimsky-Korsakov: *Scheherezade*, Op. 35 (4th movement)

Major and minor 3rds

Major and minor 3rds are important in both melody and harmony. They often occur in melodies, and chords are built up using 3rds, one on top of another.

Beethoven: Piano Sonata in B flat ('The Hammerklavier'), Op. 106

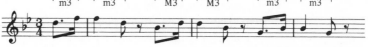

Bizet: 'Danse Bohème' from *Carmen* (Act II)

Perfect 4ths and 5ths

In melody, these intervals are often heard in fanfares and hunting-calls. They are the main intervals played by brass instruments and can provide an exciting start to a piece of music.

Wagner: *The Ride of the Valkyries*

Perfect 4ths and 5ths can be used for other effects. They are used in this example to portray the flowing and graceful movements of a swan.

Saint-Saëns: 'The Swan' from *The Carnival of Animals*

Harmonic 4ths, 5ths and 8ves have a thin and open sound.
Debussy used many of these intervals for music which is misty
and hazy.

Debussy: 'La cathédrale engloutie' from *Préludes*, Book I

Major and minor
6ths

You will often find examples of these two intervals in emotional
music – love songs, folk music, and dramatic music such as opera.
When a 6th rises it seems to stretch out with a wide swing or
leap.

Rodgers and Hammerstein: 'No Other Love' from *Victory at Sea*

No o - ther love have I___   on-ly my love for you ___

Spiritual: *Go Down Moses*

Major and minor
7ths

These intervals were banned by the church for a long time because
of their sharp, clashing sound. Perhaps one of the reasons for the
clash is that the 7th just misses being an octave, and this causes
the listener to be a little startled.

A few composers in the 16th and 17th centuries – Monteverdi
was one – decided to break this church law and used the interval
of a 7th in their music.

Monteverdi: 'Pulchra es' from *Vespers* (1610)

si   -   cut ___   Je - ru - sa - lem

Composers in the 19th and 20th centuries were fond of 7ths and used them often, especially in dramatic music.

Tchaikovsky: 'None but the Lonely Heart' from *Six Songs*, Op. 6

on - ly the sad of heart,   can tell my ang - uish

Gershwin: *An American in Paris*

Octave
(Perfect 8th)

The octave is just one semitone more than a major 7th, but its sound is entirely different. It has been used to good effect in all periods of musical composition.

Mozart: Symphony no. 29 in A

Bizet: Minuet from *L'Arlésienne Suite* no. 1

WORK ON INTERVALS (1)

1. All these intervals are from major scales. Play or sing the intervals, then

a) Give the name of the major scale which starts on the lower note

b) Describe the interval.

Example:

C major
Perfect 5th

B♭ major
Major 3rd

2. Write these intervals above and below the given notes.

Example:

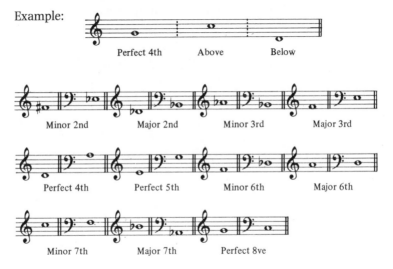

Perfect 4th   Above   Below

Minor 2nd   Major 2nd   Minor 3rd   Major 3rd

Perfect 4th   Perfect 5th   Minor 6th   Major 6th

Minor 7th   Major 7th   Perfect 8ve

3. Play or sing these melodies, then name the interval between each two notes (M = major, m = minor, P = perfect).

Delibes: 'Pizzicati' from *Sylvia* (ballet)

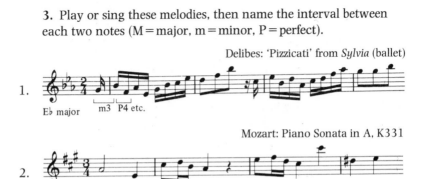

E♭ major   m3 P4 etc.

Mozart: Piano Sonata in A, K331

A major

CHAPTER TWO

The tonic and its triad

A *key* is a group or family of notes closely related to each other. The first and most important note of this family is called the *tonic*. The key and the tonic always have the same letter-name whether the key is major or minor. For example:

> in the key of C major the tonic is C
> in the key of F minor the tonic is F
> in the key of A major the tonic is A.

Role of the tonic

The tonic is always in a central role. A melody will often start on the tonic, then use other notes, but nearly always return to the tonic at the end.

In these examples, all the melodies begin and end on the tonic.

Bach: Fugue in C from *The Well-Tempered Clavier*, Book I

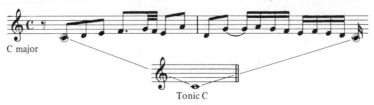

Dukas: *The Sorcerer's Apprentice*

Frère Jacques

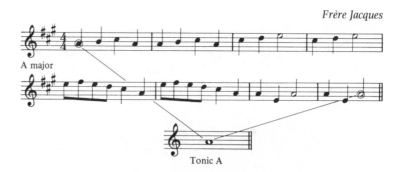

After the tonic, the next most important note of a key is the 5th, or *dominant*. The other notes – 2nd, 3rd, 4th, 6th and 7th – are less important.

A *scale* is a series of all the notes in any one key arranged in alphabetical order – a musical alphabet. It is not necessary to sound all the notes of a scale to establish the key of a piece of music. In this Minuet, only four notes of the scale are needed to establish the key of D major – D, A, F sharp and E.

Handel: Minuet II from *Music for the Royal Fireworks*

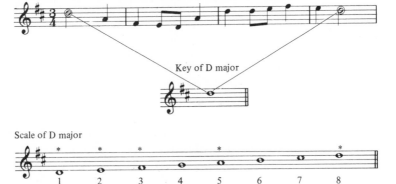

The steps of a key or scale can be seen in this diagram. Each step has its own name.

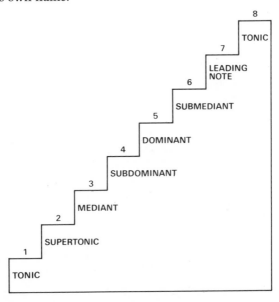

Some notes of the key are attracted to other notes. The 7th seems
to pull towards the 8th. The 2nd often wants to move towards the
tonic or 3rd. The 2nd, 4th, 6th and 7th are therefore called *active*
notes. The tonic and 3rd are *resting* notes. The 5th changes between
being an active and a resting note.

The moving and resting of notes around the tonic is called *tonality*.

Triads

For a long time music consisted of nothing more than a one-line
melody. When this was no longer enough on its own, harmony
began to develop. The earliest type of harmony was a second voice
singing a melody a 5th above or below the original melody. Both
voices sang the same melody but at a different pitch, producing
chords. A *chord* is a group of notes sounded together.

The three-note chord, called a *triad*, developed in the 13th
century. The triad has become the most commonly used chord in
music. Triads are made up of two 3rds, one sitting on top of the
other. There are two usual types of 3rd – major and minor.
A major 3rd is larger than a minor 3rd by one semitone. Compare
this with two kitchen storage jars, one larger than the other,
which stack on top of each other. They can be stacked in two
different ways.

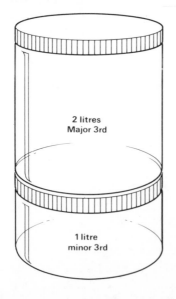

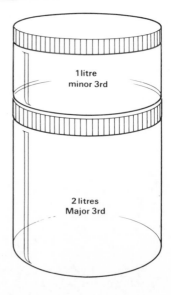

Now, think of the larger jar as a major 3rd and the smaller jar as a minor 3rd. The 3rds can also be stacked in two ways. A major 3rd with a minor 3rd stacked on top of it forms a major triad. A minor 3rd with a major 3rd stacked on top of it forms a minor triad.

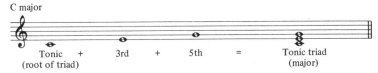

The tonic triad

The chord on note 1 – the tonic triad – is the most important of all chords.

Just as the tonic note is the most important note of melody, so the tonic chord is the centre of harmony. It is the chord from which a piece of music often starts and to which it nearly always returns at the end.

Forms and uses of the tonic triad

The notes of a chord are not always sounded together as a block chord. They may be played one after the other as a broken chord.

A triad is made up of three notes, but one or more of its notes may be duplicated at a different pitch. In this way chords can have four, five or even more notes. This is called *doubling*.

The chord remains the same however many notes are doubled, but the sound or 'colour' may alter as notes are added. Doubling can be used in a block chord or a broken chord.

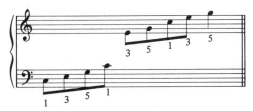

The following examples are in a variety of keys and show the tonic major chord used in different ways. The examples are all in major keys, but musical works starting with the tonic minor chord are equally common.

Handel: *Water Music*

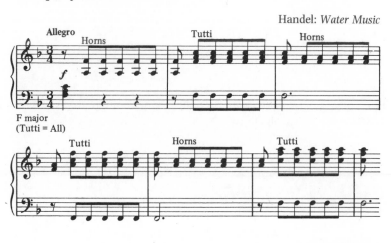

F major
(Tutti = All)

Wagner: *The Mastersingers*

C major

Smetana: 'Vltava' from *Ma vlást* (*My Country*)

C major

When the three notes of a triad are as close together as possible, the chord is said to be in *close position*. When they are spread out more, the chord is said to be in *open position*.

Close position   Open position

WORK ON THE TONIC TRIAD

1. These musical phrases start and end on a tonic note.
a) Copy out each phrase
b) Play or sing through the phrase
c) Name the tonic note and its key
d) Write out the tonic triad for each key.

Example:

Folk Song: *J'ai encore un tel pâté*

Tonic note = F   Key = F major   Tonic triad

Mozart: *Requiem*

1.

Haydn: *Emperor's Hymn*

2.

Hootchy Kootchy Dance

3.

2. The following are all tonic triads. Name the key of each.

Example:

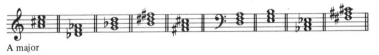

A major

3. Write the tonic chord for each of these keys: D major, A flat major, G minor, F sharp minor
a) as a block chord
b) as a broken chord
c) as a four-note chord
d) as a broken chord in a rhythm of triplets.

Example:

C major

4. Write the tonic chord for each of these keys in the following rhythmic patterns: A major, D flat major, A minor, B minor. Start and end on the tonic note.

Rhythmic patterns:

5. Compose two bugle calls using only notes of the tonic chord. Write each bugle call in a different rhythm and key.

Example:

Reveille

B♭ major.

Intervals (2)

**Augmented
4th and
diminished
5th**

In the Middle Ages composers were only allowed to use the
intervals of a 4th, 5th and octave. All other intervals were
considered unsuitable. If you play or sing almost any two notes
a 4th or 5th apart in C major, the sound will be a perfect 4th
or perfect 5th.

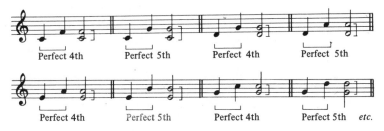

But there is one exception to this – the notes F and B. These two
notes make a sound that is far from perfect – they are called the
augmented 4th and diminished 5th.

The augmented 4th is also known as the *tritone* (three whole
tones), and the diminished 5th the *inverted tritone*. Most composers
were trained by the church in the Middle Ages, and the church
authorities made it quite clear that these two intervals were not to
be used. The augmented 4th and diminished 5th were thought to
sound so unpleasant that they were called 'diabolus in musica' –
the devil in music.

An augmented interval is one semitone larger than a perfect
interval. A diminished interval is one semitone smaller than a
perfect interval.

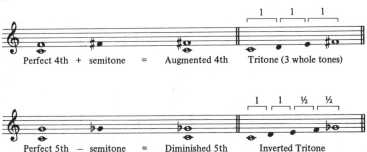

Ideas have changed about the augmented 4th and diminished 5th, but it is interesting to note that composers of the 19th and 20th centuries often used augmented and diminished intervals when writing music about evil or the supernatural.

Musorgsky: *A Night on the Bare Mountain*

A witches' Sabbath

Stravinsky: *Firebird Suite*

The evil magician moves . . . .

**Compound
intervals**

So far we have looked at intervals of less than an octave. These are called *simple* intervals. Intervals of more than an octave are called *compound*. An octave is a repetition of the same note eight notes higher or lower. A compound interval adds eight notes to a simple interval. A 9th is like a simple 2nd; a 10th is like a simple 3rd; and so on.

In harmony a 10th serves much the same purpose as a 3rd. In melody, however, simple and compound intervals are rather different. Play two notes a 3rd apart, followed by the same two notes a 10th apart. You will notice that the compound interval sounds more empty and open.

Compound intervals also help to make melodies more emotional and intense. Listen to these examples of compound intervals and compare them with the sounds of simple intervals.

Beethoven: String Quartet in F, Op. 135 (1st movement)

Minor 9th

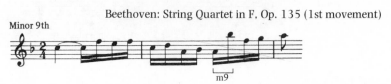

Beethoven: *Grosse Fuge* in B flat for string quartet, Op. 133

Minor 10th

Saint-Saëns: *Marche héroïque*, Op. 34

Major 10th

Jazz chords (harmonic intervals)

13ths

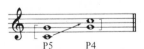

Chopin: Scherzo in B minor, Op. 20

Inverted intervals

Intervals can be *inverted* (turned upside down). Any two intervals which form an octave when added together are called inversions of each other. To invert an interval, one of the notes must be put an octave higher or lower. In other words, the bottom note changes places with the top note.

All inverted intervals add up to 9.
A 2nd when inverted becomes a 7th $(2 + 7 = 9)$
A 3rd when inverted becomes a 6th $(3 + 6 = 9)$
A 4th when inverted becomes a 5th $(4 + 5 = 9)$
A 5th when inverted becomes a 4th $(5 + 4 = 9)$
A 6th when inverted becomes a 3rd $(6 + 3 = 9)$
A 7th when inverted becomes a 2nd $(7 + 2 = 9)$

When an interval is inverted its quality also changes, except in the case of perfect intervals.

A perfect interval when inverted stays perfect.
A major interval when inverted becomes minor.
A minor interval when inverted becomes major.
An augmented interval when inverted becomes diminished.
A diminished interval when inverted becomes augmented.

Perfect stays Perfect   Major becomes Minor   Minor becomes Major

Augmented becomes Diminished   Diminished becomes Augmented

This simple diagram will help to make this point clear.

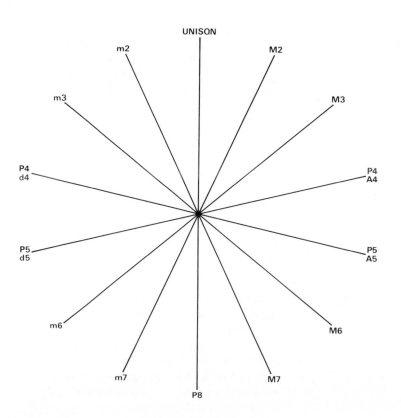

So far we have looked at each interval separately. Music, of course, is made up of many intervals.

We would expect a leap of a 6th to be more forceful than a leap of a 3rd, because the distance is greater. But two exceptions are the augmented 4th and major 7th. Both of these intervals are very energetic, and both are more forceful than some larger intervals (e.g. a major 7th is more forceful than an octave).

But as a general rule:

1. Chromatic intervals are usually more forceful than larger diatonic intervals, because they have a note or notes which are not part of the key.

2. A rising interval is generally more forceful than a falling interval.

3. The effect of intervals is governed by the music. A 4th, for example, would be more forceful in music consisting of smaller intervals than in music with larger intervals.

This passage becomes more forceful as the intervals become larger.

Beethoven: Symphony no. 5 in C minor

WORK ON INTERVALS (2)

1. Write out these melodies, then play or sing them. Mark the perfect 4ths and perfect 5ths.

Example:

Mozart: *The Magic Flute*

Bach: Fugue in E flat from *The Well-Tempered Clavier*, Book II

Schubert: Symphony no. 9 in C

Mark the augmented 4th in this melody.

Chopin: Mazurka in F sharp minor, Op. 6 no. 1

Mark the diminished 5th in this melody.

Bach: *St Matthew Passion*

2. Write the following compound intervals above each of these notes, as shown in the example.

Minor 9th   Major 10th   Perfect 11th   Major 9th   Minor 10th   Perfect 12th

3. Copy these musical extracts, then mark the compound intervals and describe each.

Bach: Concerto in D minor for 2 violins

3.

Stravinsky: Violin Concerto in D

4.

4. Write the inversions of these intervals, then describe both the interval and its inversion.

Example:

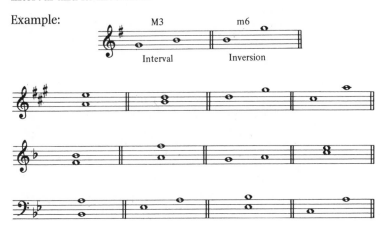

M = Major
m = minor
A = Augmented
d = diminished

CHAPTER THREE

The dominant and its triad

After the tonic, the dominant is the most important note of a scale. Intervals follow an order which is quite natural and mathematical. When a note is sounded we hear a mixture of sounds – the main note itself, plus a number of faint sounds. These faint sounds are called *overtones* or *harmonics*.

This diagram shows the first 12 overtones that it is possible to get from the note C. Every other note has its own set of overtones, with intervals in the same proportions.

OVERTONES OF C

Notice these points:

1. The note sounded (called the *fundamental*) is the lowest note. The overtones are higher sounds.
2. The perfect intervals (8ve, 5th and 4th) are the lowest sounds in the overtone series. These are the overtones most easily heard by many people.
3. The fundamental and the interval of a 5th or 12th above occur more often than any other overtone. This helps to explain why the dominant note is the most important after the tonic.

Composers have often used the overtone series of notes in their music. Notice the similarity between this music by Richard Strauss and the overtones of F. Only the notes marked * are not in the overtone series of F.

OVERTONES OF F

R. Strauss: *Till Eulenspiegel*, Op. 28

Another composer, Chopin, wrote arpeggios in his piano music which are almost identical to the overtone series of the lowest notes in the music.

In melody, the notes 1–5–1 establish the key of a piece of music. The tonic is a stable or resting note, but the dominant seems to want to move on to another note, often the tonic. Play or sing this example and stop when you reach the dominant note. The music will sound unfinished. The phrase only sounds complete when you move on and come to rest on the tonic.

Trad. Song: *All Through the Night*

Dominant

The dominant triad

The dominant triad is major and is made up of the 5th, 7th and 9th notes of the scale, in that order.

1 2 3 4 5 6 7 8 9 10   5 + 7 + 9   =   Dominant triad
                                 (root)   (major)

Just as the dominant note seems to want to move on to a resting note, the dominant chord acts in the same way by pulling towards the tonic chord. The move from an active to a resting chord is called a *resolution*.

The 3rd of the dominant chord is also the leading note of the scale, and the leading note is the most active note of any scale. Play or sing any scale and hear the strong pull of the leading note to the tonic.

Just as the tonic triad can be written in a number of different ways (for example, as a block chord, a broken chord and with notes doubled), the same is true of the dominant triad.

DOMINANT TRIADS

Block chord   Broken chord   Root doubled   Root and 3rd doubled

The tonic (I) and dominant (V) triads are the most natural chords in music. Many tunes have been harmonised with just these two chords. The progression of chords I to V and V to I is found in all types of music, from early to modern times.

(a)   Purcell: Suite no. 8 in F

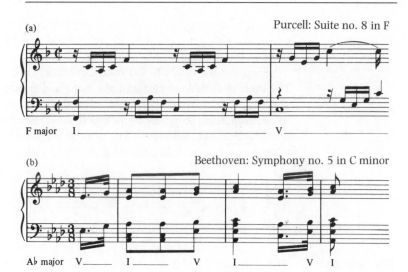

F major   I _____ V _____

(b)   Beethoven: Symphony no. 5 in C minor

A♭ major   V _____ I _____ V   I _____ V   I

Martini: *Plaisir d'amour*

(c)

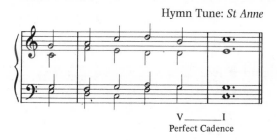

G major   I _____   V _____   I _____

In written language, a resting place is marked by a full stop.
When music comes to a resting point a *cadence* is used. The most
commonly used cadence is chord V followed by chord I – the
perfect cadence. Examples of the perfect cadence can be found in
almost any piece of music. Here is just one example:

Hymn Tune: *St Anne*

V _____ I
Perfect Cadence

Harmonic movement

In harmonic progressions roman numerals (for example, I and V) are used for chords, arabic numerals (for example, 1 and 5) are used for single notes.

When chord I moves to chord V (or V to I), the movement of the notes should be close and smooth. Notice in this example how the top line has the common note of both chords, G. This forms a link between the chords. The middle and bottom parts each move down just one note, then back.

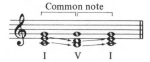

It is a good idea to keep the common note in the same part or voice. This makes smooth movement and links the chords together well.

German Folk Song: *O, once I went a-walking*

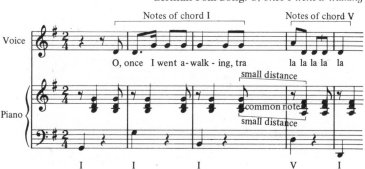

Notice also the following things from this example:

1. When a note or group of notes belongs to the tonic chord, it is harmonised with that chord (I). The same applies to notes from the dominant chord – chord V is used.
2. When the notes of a melody form a broken chord, the chord under them stays the same.
3. The parts move only small distances to make smooth harmony.

Let us suppose you are going to add chords I or V to a simple folk tune. You have already learnt that when the melody has a note which is from chord I you will use chord I as the harmony. If the melody has a note which is from chord V then this chord will be used. But how do you harmonise note 5, which is common to both chords? You will see that when the tune jumps to and from notes of the same chord, then that chord stays under the tune, even if one of the notes could be harmonised with either chord I or V. The only time when this is not a good idea is if the music sounds boring because the same chord has been used over and over again.

Czech Folk Tune (arr. Rezniček)

* = Common note

This folk song could be harmonised by using just the tonic chord.

French Folk Song: *As-tu vu la casquette?*

* = Common note

If you listen to this version the harmony soon becomes tiring.
Note 5, common to both chords, could provide us with the chance
of using chord V, instead of using chord I throughout.

French Folk Song: *As-tu vu la casquette?*

This version has much greater variety and more movement.

WORK ON THE DOMINANT TRIAD

1. Write out these dominant triads and name the key for each.

G major

2. Write the chord progression I–V–I in the following keys: C major, D major, F major, A major.
Keep the common note in the same part and move the other parts as little as possible.

3. Copy out this well-known tune. Fill in the notes needed to complete each tonic or dominant triad at the points marked with a * (the first two notes have been done for you).

Pop goes the Weasel

4. All the notes of this Hungarian folk melody can be harmonised with either chord I or V in G major. Copy out the tune, then under each note add two more notes to complete the triads. The first bar has been done for you.

Melodic shape

So far, you have looked at melody as movement in steps and leaps over a small, medium or wide range of notes. There is another important feature of melody writing – its shape or outline. Knowledge of melodic shape is important because:

1. It will help you to understand the *overall* pattern of a melody.
2. The shapes will act as frameworks for your own melodies.
3. You will begin to think of melody in long lines, rather than as one note moving to another note.
4. When writing chord progressions it is important that the bass as well as the soprano melody has a good shape or outline. Understanding shape in melody will also help you to write good, flowing bass parts.

Here are some of the more common shapes seen in melody through the ages. Composers, of course, are individual people, and it will not always be possible to fit their melodies into particular patterns. Nevertheless, the study of melodic shapes is a valuable guide for composing your own melodies.

1. The wave

With small rises and falls, the music will usually be gentle and flowing. As the waves become larger, the music will often be more intense, but still flowing.
　　This plainsong melody follows the gentle wave pattern.

Adoro te devote (Mode V)

Wave-shaped melody with quite sharp peaks:

Chopin: Nocturne in D flat, Op. 27 no. 2

Wave-shaped melody in popular music:

Rodgers and Hammerstein: 'Oh, what a beautiful mornin'' from *Oklahoma!*

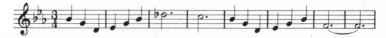

Sometimes you will hear melody which moves backwards and forwards in a wave pattern, but then reaches a climax. This climax often comes right at the end of the phrase:

Prokofiev: *Classical Symphony* (3rd movement)

2. The ascending wave

This shape gradually rises, falls back a little, rises again, until an exciting climax is reached. When the climax occurs it is like waves breaking on to the seashore. When their energy is spent, the melody falls away for the last time.

Elgar: *Variations on a Original Theme* ('Nimrod')

3. The descending wave

Similar to the ascending wave, but in the opposite direction. This type of melody is often gentle in mood but can be quite exciting at times.

Neapolitan Folk Song: *Santa Lucia*

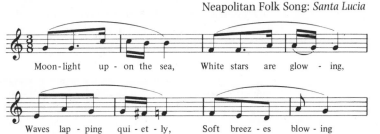

4. The hill

The melody curves up to the top of the hill where there is a climax, then falls away.

Grieg: 'Solveig's Song' from *Peer Gynt*

5. The valley

The melodic curve starts on a high point, moves down to a lower note, then rises again in a flowing curve to approximately the pitch of the first note.

Haydn: *The Creation*

low note

6. The upward slope

One of the simplest of musical shapes, the upward slope is really just a scale. But in the hands of a skilful composer and written in different rhythms, this pattern can produce interesting and exciting music.

Bach: *Italian Concerto*

7. The downward slope

This shape again could be difficult to make interesting, but composers have used the descending slope to good effect in their music.

Berlioz: *Symphonie fantastique* ('March to the Scaffold')

8. The straight level

Straight-line melody is often used with words or with changing harmonies. Sooner or later the melody moves to other notes, when the desired effect has been achieved.

Khachaturian: Sabre Dance from *Gayaneh*

These are the basic shapes of melody. Often a melody will use a combination of two or more shapes. This melody uses a mixture of the descending wave and upward slope.

Saint-Saëns: 'The Swan' from *The Carnival of Animals*

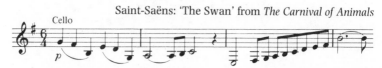

Some musical phrases consist of small curves and other patterns, but if these are seen as one general shape, the result is a large overall curve.

Liszt: *Hungarian Rhapsody* no. 2 (transposed)

WORK ON MELODIC SHAPE

1. Write out the following musical examples, then:
a) Play or sing through the melody
b) Give the name of a melodic shape which fits the melody
c) Put a circle round the highest and lowest note(s)
d) Mark the climax with a *
e) Describe the range of notes used as small, medium or wide.

Musorgsky: *A Night on the Bare Mountain*

1.

Liszt: *Dante Symphony*

2.

Handel: *Music for the Royal Fireworks* (Minuet)

3.

Wagner: Siegfried's Horn Call from *Götterdämmerung*

4.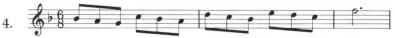

Beethoven: Symphony no. 1 in C

5.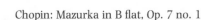

Vivaldi: 'Winter' from *The Four Seasons*

6.

2. These melodies use two or more melodic shapes. Name the shapes and the range of notes used.

Chopin: Mazurka in B flat, Op. 7 no. 1

7.

Berlioz: *Symphonie fantastique* (5th movement)

8.

3. Write short melodies of your own in simple keys for each of the melodic shapes mentioned in the chapter.

Harmony in four parts

The practice of writing harmony in four parts developed in the 15th and 16th centuries. The Reformation in the 16th century was a religious revolution which gave rise to the Protestant Church.
It had a great influence upon music throughout Europe. The main figure of the Reformation was Martin Luther. He was concerned that church-goers should take a more active part in the services. One of the ways in which they could do this was by singing the tunes of chorales (German hymn tunes), while the choir added the harmonies. Four-part harmony now began to take shape.

   Four-part harmony was designed to fit the ranges of the human voice – soprano, alto, tenor and bass – and it gives a good balance to the sound of a chord.

   How do we write in four parts when there are only three notes in a triad? The answer is simple. One of the three notes is doubled. Play these two examples and you will notice that the four-part version doubles the root of each chord.

4-part harmony (roots doubled)

        I   V   I

Four-part harmony can be written for the piano or other groups of instruments, but it is more usual to think of the parts as voices.
The comfortable range (or compass) of the average voice in each of the four categories is:

        Soprano   Alto   Tenor   Bass

Notes outside these ranges should be used only if:

1. A special effect is needed, such as a big climax.
2. No other note is suitable.

The soprano and alto parts are written on the treble stave, and the tenor and bass on the bass stave. Stems of notes go up for the soprano and tenor, down for the alto and bass.

Let us now look at a few examples of four-part writing.

Vivaldi: *Gloria* (voice parts only)

It is interesting to note from this short example that:

1. Each of the four voices (SATB) has notes well within its own range.

2. The voices do not cross or overlap each other.

3. The root of each chord is doubled.

4. The chords are complete – each one has a root, 3rd and 5th.

5. The distance between soprano and alto, alto and tenor, tenor and bass is never more than an octave.

6. The common note (A) of chords I and V is in the same part.

7. When the chord changes, the soprano and alto move the smallest possible distance.

8. The bass moves a greater distance – this is the part which indicates the chord changes.

9. There are no intervals used which are difficult to sing – for example, 7ths, or augmented or diminished intervals.

Most of these points are also true of the following carol.

Dorset Carol (traditional)

(*This note is a tone outside the normal soprano range, but it is occasionally better to do this to preserve the melodic flow than to stick rigidly to the range)

But notice also that:

1. At (a) the 5th of the chord is doubled rather than the root. In traditional harmony the 5th may be doubled or even left out altogether (b). The 3rd of a chord should never be left out.

2. The tenor and bass sing the root as a unison note at (c).

3. The chord changes help to establish the $\frac{6}{8}$ metre by changing mostly on the 1st and 4th quaver beats, and across the bar.

4. This carol uses a new method of harmonising at (d). The parts change notes but keep the tonic chord. When the alto moves from note 3 to 5, the tenor moves from 1 to 3 so that the 3rd is not left out.

5. The soprano is the most tuneful and active part.

6. There are two notes in the soprano which help to give the carol a flowing style (e). These notes could be harmonised with chord I, but the music would lose some of its smooth and flowing movement. These are called *embellishing* notes.

7. When the bass is not changing its note, the other voices sometimes all leap in the same direction (f).

8. The leading note is not doubled (g).

9. The distance between the tenor and bass is more than an octave at (h). This sounds satisfactory – it is usually better to have large intervals at the bottom of a chord than at the top. More than an octave between soprano and alto can sound awkward.

When to change the chord

In traditional music, composers usually change the harmony according to the metre, on strong beats. Metre is the basic plan of note values and accents, which stay the same throughout a piece or section of a piece. The beats are grouped into patterns, decided at the start by the time signature used.

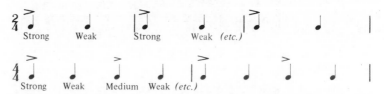

Suppose the following melody is to be harmonised using chords I or V.

The first bar can only be harmonised using I.
The second bar can only be harmonised using V.
Bars 3 and 4 present a problem because of the common note (G). We could use chord V for the first note of bar 3, then change to chord I for the last two notes.

But the harmony sounds weak in bars 3 and 4 because the chords do not change across the bar line.

This version sounds much better because the chords now fit the $\frac{2}{4}$ metre.

To write good harmony it is necessary:

1. To select the right chords and use them in the correct rhythm.
2. To have smooth and independent part-writing.

There are three main ways of making voice parts interesting.

1. Contrary motion

The parts move in opposite directions.

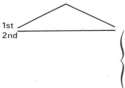

Bach: *Italian Concerto*

2. Oblique motion

One part remains on the same note while the other part moves.

Bach: *Two-Part Invention* no. 4

3. Similar motion

Both parts move in the same direction but not using the same intervals.

Handel: *Water Music*

When two parts move in the same direction keeping the same interval apart, this is called *parallel* motion. Good part-writing often rules out the use of parallel motion, except by the intervals of a 3rd or 6th.

It is not possible for all harmony to follow these three types of movement. As you become more familiar with the study of harmony, you will notice that the soprano and bass are often more independent and interesting than the two inside parts. It takes a lot of skill to make all the parts equally interesting. Bach was a master of this in his harmonisation of chorale melodies.

WORK ON FOUR-PART HARMONY

1. Add parts for ATB below each of these soprano notes to make four-part chords. Write two arrangements for each.

2. Add parts for SAT above each of these bass notes. Write three different arrangements for each.

3. Which note has been doubled in these chords?

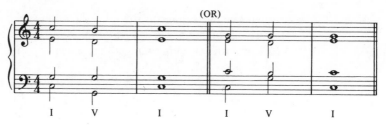

4. Write the progression I–V–I in four-part harmony in the following keys: G major, D major, A flat major.
Double the root of each chord and keep the common note (5) in the same part throughout.

Example:

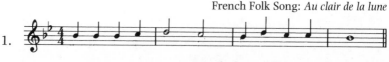

Sing and play your answers.

5. Harmonise the following melodies in four parts.
When deciding whether to use I or V for the common note, change chords across the bar line and on strong accents where possible.

French Folk Song: *Au clair de la lune*

1.

Appalachian Folk Song: *Bye, Bye, Baby*

2.

6. Make a list of the weak points in this harmonisation.

Composing melodies

Composers have written little about how they compose melodies.
Many people imagine that a melody springs readily to a composer's
mind. Sometimes this does happen, but often composers have
struggled with many versions of a tune before being satisfied.
Beethoven often found composing melodies difficult. He said:
'I change many things, discard, and try again until I am satisfied.'
The finished melody of the *Adagio un poco mosso* from his Piano
Concerto no. 5 in E flat (Op. 73) went through many changes
before Beethoven was happy with the result. Here are just two of
the early sketches:

As you will notice, the final version of this flowing and beautiful
tune contains some of the ideas from his early sketches.

Beethoven: Piano Concerto no. 5 in E flat (2nd movement)

There is, without doubt, a gift in creating melodies such as this.
But a study of melody writing will certainly help us understand
more about the skill involved.

Melodic ideas   It is essential that a melody has unity of idea. Often a person
will come up with several good ideas for a tune, but it is important
that these ideas are closely related, well-balanced and part of the
whole scheme.

The difference between the amateur and professional is often all
too obvious here. The amateur may have some very good ideas,
and for this reason does not want to change a single note of his
creation. The professional, on the other hand, looks at his melody
and questions the result. Does it fit together well? Perhaps this

section could be left out or changed in some way; that interval is not right; a more gradual climax is needed here; and so on.

Melodic climax

Most melodies have a point to aim for – a climax – followed by a resting-place. (The exceptions to this are downward-sloping, straight-level and wave-pattern shapes.)

Mozart: Serenade in E flat, K375

A climax uses a number of ingredients to make its point – harmony, rhythm and volume – but the most obvious is the highest note in the melody. This high note should be used sparingly (often only once), otherwise the climax will lose its impact.

Berlioz: *Overture: Roman Carnival*

Repeated climax

This type of climax, where the highest note is repeated several times, needs skilful handling. Composers sometimes repeat the highest note several times to avoid a real climax, so that the melody is more gentle.

Song: *Amazing Grace*

The repeated high note is also used for exactly the opposite effect – to make the climax even more forceful and dramatic.

Prokofiev: 'Troika' from *Lieutenant Kijé Suite*

Melodic cadences

All melodies need a moment of pause or rest. A tune without rest is like language without punctuation. The pause or rest will usually take place:
a) on a longer-value note, or
b) on a longer-value note followed by a rest sign.

There are two ways of ending a melodic phrase:
a) on the tonic note (a perfect cadence), or
b) on a note other than the tonic (an incomplete cadence).

This example ends on a longer-value note and has an incomplete cadence. This is rather like the pause that a comma provides in the middle of a sentence.

Humperdinck: *Overture: Hansel and Gretel*

This example ends with a longer-value note followed by a rest.

Bizet: 'Toreador's Song' from *Carmen*

Here the phrase ends on a longer-value note (the tonic) and makes a perfect cadence.

Warlock: *Capriol Suite* (5th movement)

Melodic movement

All melodies must move up or down. Every instrument and voice has a limited range of notes, so a melody must at some time turn round and move in the other direction.

Throughout musical history, composers have followed three simple ideas for this up-and-down movement.

a) After a wide leap, the melody turns back and moves by step:

Schubert: *Overture: Rosamunde*

Mozart: *Requiem*

Large leap Step back

A wide leap creates drama and excitement, while a small movement by step in the opposite direction provides relief.

b) After a number of small leaps in the same direction, the melody moves by step in the opposite direction.

Beethoven: Symphony no. 1 in C

Small leaps   Step back

c) After a scale passage, the melody often moves in the opposite direction.

Mahler: Symphony no. 1 in D

pp   Scale passage   Opposite direction

Points to remember

1. Good melody should be well-balanced, with a good shape and unity of style.

2. Melody should have movement, then resting-places.

3. Avoid using the same note too often.

4. Avoid using too many different rhythms and ideas – all music should have some repetition.

5. Avoid movement in the same direction after leaps or scale passages.

6. Study, sing and play melodies in the styles which you like, be they jazz, pop, classical or modern music. Then try writing your own melodies.

7. Include with your melody some directions for dynamics (volume) and tempo (speed), whether it is for voice or instrument, as well as phrase marks. All these points can affect the style of your melody.

WORK ON COMPOSING MELODIES

1. Answer the phrases with a balancing phrase of the same length.

2. One of the following melodies is by Mozart, and the other is by a young person who has just started composing tunes. Who, in your opinion, is the composer of each? Give reasons for your choice by listing the strong and weak points of each melody.

3. Write three simple melodies, each eight bars in length. Use only the notes of chords I and V in the key you choose.

The first melody should be wave-shaped with the climax note used only once.

For the second melody use a number of small leaps followed by steps in the opposite direction.

Your third melody should include a scale passage.

The subdominant chord

The tonic and dominant chords are the most important in any key, but there is another chord – the subdominant (IV) – which is also very important. These three chords (I, IV and V) are called the *primary* triads. All other chords (II, III, VI and VII) are called *secondary* – that is, second in importance.

Chords I and V are used a great deal in harmony, but examples of music which use only these two chords are difficult to find. By adding the subdominant chord to our list, we use all the notes of a scale.

The subdominant triad is made up of the 4th, 6th and 8th degrees of a scale.

If we compare the progression I–IV with V–I, you will see that in both the roots fall by a 5th.

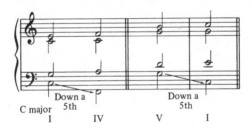

This shows how the tonic is the very heart of a key. Chords IV and V lie either side of it and are strongly attracted to it. Using the three chords close together is the strongest way of stating the key or tonality of a piece.

Hymn Tune: *Petra*

Harmonic movement of I, IV and V

In order to obtain the smoothest movement from IV to I, the common note (1) is kept in the same voice. The other parts move only small distances.

IV moving to V is more difficult for two reasons:

a) the two chords have no common note, and

b) they are only one tone apart, which can easily create parallel 5ths. Parallel 5ths should only be used for special effects as the sound they produce is rather bare.

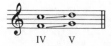

One of the best ways of moving from IV to V or from V to IV is to use contrary motion. The upper voices (SAT) move small distances upwards or downwards, and the bass moves by step in the opposite direction.

Ebeling: *All my Heart* (carol)

Cadences using IV, V and I

The progression IV–V–I is the most decisive way of ending a piece. For this reason it is not often used in the middle of a phrase.

Purcell: *Dido and Aeneas*

It is possible to make a perfect cadence sound less final by using
the 3rd or 5th (rather than the tonic) in the soprano voice. Used
like this, the perfect cadence is suitable when there is more music
to follow.

Responses in E

This is not the only way to make a phrase sound less final.
The imperfect cadence sounds far from complete, as it comes to
rest on V, often by way of chord I.

Hymn Tune: *Moscow*

The imperfect cadence is often used at a midway point in
harmonising a melody, with the perfect cadence coming at the end
of the following phrase. It is a kind of half-way house, a temporary
resting-place.

Bach: *St Matthew Passion*

There is another cadence which does not use chord V at all. This cadence consists of IV moving to I and is called *plagal*. The plagal cadence sounds less forceful than the perfect or imperfect types. If a peaceful or gentle end to a phrase is required, then this is the cadence to use. It is often included at the end of hymns for singing 'A-men'.

Hymn Tune: *Hanover*

Harmonising melodies with I, IV and V

Many traditional, folk and pop songs use only I, IV and V for their harmony. These three chords are the backbone of many compositions.

Foster: *The Old Folks at Home*

After playing or singing through *Old Folks at Home*, note the following points about the way in which the harmony is written:

1. The tonic note can be harmonised with either I or IV. Chord I is used at (a), as it is better to keep the same chord when the melody leaps.
2. The melody note at (b) is from IV, so the harmony has to change here. This chord change is also in keeping with the $\frac{4}{4}$ metre because there is a medium stress on the third beat of the bar.

3. The common note stays in the alto voice when the chord changes from I to IV, (a) to (b).

4. When the chord stays the same for a complete bar (c), the voice parts have some variety by exchanging notes.

5. When the melody moves to the 3rd (c), the alto moves to the tonic to avoid doubling the 3rd.

6. The alto moves to the tonic at (d) and (e) so that the leading note can rise. The root in both these cases is tripled and the 5th left out.

WORK ON THE SUBDOMINANT CHORD

1. Write chord IV (in four parts) in these keys: G major, E major,
E flat major, F major.
Give three arrangements for each. Remember to construct the chords
from the bass upwards.

Example:

C major

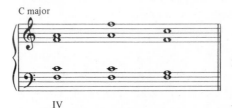

IV

2. Write plagal cadences (IV–I) in the following keys. Use chords
in close or open position, but keep the common note (1) in the
same part and move the other voices as little as possible.
   D major, A major, B flat major, D flat major.

3. Write the progressions IV to V and V to IV in the same keys
as in question 1. Use contrary motion, with the bass moving
upwards and SAT moving downwards.

4. Copy out these two short extracts, then name the chords used.
Write Roman numerals for the chords underneath the bass line.

Batten: *When the Lord turned again*

1.

F minor

Bull: *The King's Hunting Jigg*

2.

G major

5. This Canadian folk song can be harmonised throughout with I,
IV and V chords. Indicate the chords you would use by writing
Roman numerals under the stave.

Folk Song: *Un canadien errant*

Example: I   I

6. Harmonise this melody in four parts (adding ATB), using I, IV or V where appropriate.

Playford: *The English Dancing Master*

Scales and modes

The *modes* are old scales that were used in Europe in Medieval times. They are sometimes called the *church modes* because the early melody of the church (called *plainsong*) is written in the modes. Many well-known songs are also composed in these old modes, and composers from early to modern times have been interested in using them in their compositions.

The order of tones (T) and semitones (S) decides the type of scale. A major scale has semitones between 3–4 and 7–8.

A harmonic minor scale has semitones between 2–3, 5–6 and 7–8.

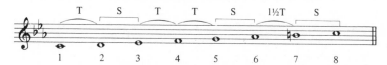

A melodic minor scale has semitones between 2–3 and 7–8 when ascending, and between 6–5 and 3–2 when descending.

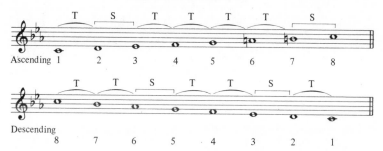

Modes

These examples of the six most common modes show where the semitones (S) occur. The tonic of a mode is called the *final*. It is sometimes necessary to change the pitch of a mode by starting on a different note. This sometimes happens in songs when the notes of the mode would be too high or low for the singer. Any mode can start on any note, but it is important when transposing modes that the order of tones and semitones stays the same.

Dorian mode   (D to D)

This mode was often used for plainsong melody and folk tunes.

What shall we do with the drunken sailor?

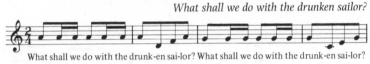

What shall we do with the drunk-en sai-lor? What shall we do with the drunk-en sai-lor?

What shall we do with the drunk-en sai - lor Ear - ly in the morn - ing?

Phrygian mode   (E to E)

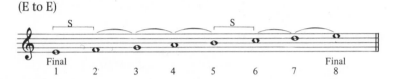

This mode has a strong pull downwards because of its 'flattened' note (*) in the bottom of the mode.

Chorale *Aus tiefer Noth*

flattened
2nd

Lydian mode   (F to F)

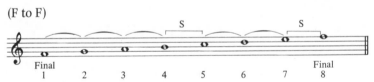

An unusual mode in that it starts with three whole tones. It is used a great deal in Polish folk music.

Musorgsky: Polacca from *Boris Godunov*

Transposed mode

This mode has been transposed to run from C to C, but the order of tones and semitones remains the same (semitones between 4–5, 7–8).

Mixolydian mode (G to G)

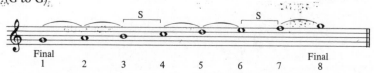

Final 1   2   3   4   5   6   7   Final 8

This mode has a bright quality. The American square-dance tune *Old Joe Clarke* is in a transposed version of this mode.

Old Joe Clarke

Transposed mode

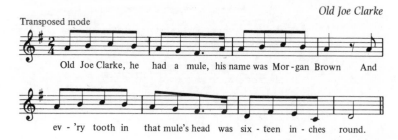

Old Joe Clarke, he   had a   mule, his name was Mor-gan Brown   And

ev - 'ry   tooth in   that mule's head was six - teen   in - ches   round.

Aeolian mode   (A to A)

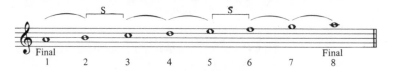

Final 1   2   3   4   5   6   7   Final 8

Somerset Folk Song: *Farewell, my dearest Nancy*

Transposed mode

Ionian mode   (C to C)

Final 1   2   3   4   5   6   7   Final 8

This mode is the same as a major scale.

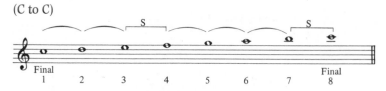

Pentatonic scale

This is a very old scale, some say from long before the modes. It is really just a shortened version of our major scale. It has five different notes – *pente* in Greek means 'five'. All its notes are a whole tone or more apart. Here is one example of this scale:

It is interesting to note that this scale has exactly the same intervals between its notes as the black notes on the piano.

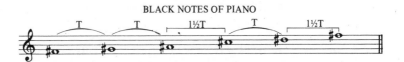

The pentatonic scale has been used for Asian, African, Scottish and other European melodies. It is almost a universal scale.

Auld Lang Syne

WORK ON SCALES AND MODES

1. Write the six most common modes starting on the notes C, G and F.

You will need to use accidentals for the correct order of tones and semitones. Sing or play your answers as you write.

Example:

⌒ = tone   S = semitone

2. Write three versions of the pentatonic scale starting on D, A and B flat.

3. Write out these melodies, then play or sing through them several times. Name the mode or scale in which each is written. It will help you to decide the mode or scale if you mark where the semitones occur.

Musorgsky: *Boris Godunov*

Gregorian Chant Sequence: *Victimae paschali laudes*

Vi - cti - mae pa - scha - li   lau - des   im - mo - lent Chri - sti - a - ni

Hebridean Folk Tune: *The Coolin' of Rum*

Somerset Folk Tune: *O Sally, my dear*

Hymn Tune

5.

Dvořák: Symphony no. 9 in E minor (2nd movement)

6.

4. Compose two short melodies (about eight bars in length) using a different mode for each. It is important to use the tonic note (final), the tonic triad notes, and other characteristic notes of the mode near the beginning of your tunes.

5. Write two short melodies using only notes from a pentatonic scale.

CHAPTER SIX

Embellishing notes

In our study of harmony so far, we have thought of the notes in
a melody as being part of a chord. When the melody moves to a
different note the harmony moves with it. But this is not always
the case, as we shall discover. Music is made more interesting when
the melody sometimes goes its own way before teaming up with the
harmony again. These independent notes which are not harmonised
are known as *embellishing* notes.

John Brown's Body

* = notes not included in the chord below

'Embellish' means to make beautiful with ornaments, or to increase
interest by adding some extra detail. This is exactly what these
notes do – they are extra detail which makes the music more
interesting.

There are several ways in which embellishing notes may appear
in music.

Passing notes

These are notes which link up the melody between one harmonic
note and another. They help the melody to move smoothly, and
make it no longer necessary to change the harmony with every
note change in the melody.

The First Nowell

H = Harmony note   * = Passing note

*Unaccented
passing notes*

Notice that the passing notes mainly come on weak beats or
between beats.

In the following example, the first bar moves down a scale,
outlining the chord of D minor. Between each of the notes of this
chord there are passing notes.

Bach: Prelude in D minor from *The Well-Tempered Clavier*, Book II

Strong beats

* = Passing note

D minor   Outline of chord

Double passing notes

Passing notes can also occur in two or more parts at once.

Handel: Pastoral Symphony from *Messiah*

* = Double passing notes

Accented passing notes

These are much the same as other passing notes. An accented passing note occurs in stepwise movement, but, as its name suggests, it comes on the beat or accent rather than in between beats. It creates a clash (dissonance) with the chord that accompanies it.

Mozart: Piano Sonata in A minor, K310

* = Accented passing note

Auxiliary notes

This is another type of embellishing note which moves one step up or down and then returns to the original note.

The Zither Carol (Czech Folk Tune)

Girls and boys, leave your toys, make no noise

* = Auxiliary note

Auxiliary notes may occur in two or more parts at the same time.

Silent Night

Si - lent night,   Ho - ly night
* = Auxiliary notes in two parts

Sometimes the notes both above and below are used before returning to the original note. These are called *changing notes*.

Beethoven: Symphony no. 8 in F

† * M   † * M   † * M

M = Main note
† = Step down
* = Step up

Turn

A more elaborate pattern of embellishing notes is the *turn*. A sign is often used for the turn, but sometimes the notes are written out in full. The sign shows the shape which the notes follow.

M = Main note

M   M   M

The turn consists of the main note, the note above, the main note, the note below and the main note again. This example shows the turn written out in full, without the sign.

Mozart: Piano Sonata in C minor, K457

Turn

The inverted turn follows much the same pattern, but the order of notes is turned upside down (inverted).

See the example at the top of the next page.

Mozart: Piano Sonata in C minor, K457

INVERTED TURN

Inverted turn

Appoggiatura   'Appoggiatura' is an Italian word for a 'leaning' note. The appoggiatura sounds rather like a wrong note followed by the right one. It is a note one step above or below the main note which takes the place of the main note in the chord. It then moves to the note of the chord, giving the impression of leaning on this note.

* = Appoggiatura — taking the place of the main note

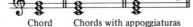

Chord   Chords with appoggiaturas

Appoggiaturas and accented passing notes are very similar. The only difference is that the appoggiatura is approached by a leap and the accented passing note by a step. This example shows the difference quite clearly.

Bach: Gavotte from French Suite no. 5

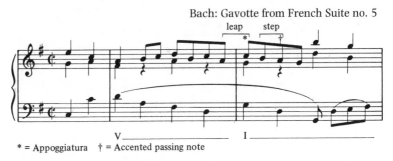

* = Appoggiatura   † = Accented passing note

The appoggiatura generally sounds better when the resolution note is not used in another voice at the same time as the appoggiatura itself. Play these two examples and notice how much better the effect is when the resolution note is not doubled.

Not doubled   Doubled

Appoggiaturas usually lean on the main note from above. A more unusual effect is obtained with the lower appoggiatura – this rises to the resolution note.

Tchaikovsky: Piano Concerto no. 1 in B flat minor (1st movement)

* = Appoggiatura rising to resolution note

Appoggiaturas can occur in two, three or more voices at the same time. These are called double and triple appoggiaturas.

Mozart: Symphony no. 25 in G minor

* = Double appoggiatura

Bach: *St Matthew Passion*

* = Triple appoggiatura

Anticipation

An anticipation is the sounding of a note on a weak beat before it becomes a harmony note on the next beat. The note arrives in one voice before the rest of the chord sounds in the other voices. This type of embellishing note was very popular with 16th- and 17th-century composers.

Morley: *Now is the month of maying*

* = Anticipation

WORK ON EMBELLISHING NOTES

1. Label the different types of embellishing notes in these extracts.

Folk Song: *Three Ravens*

Handel: Sarabande from Suite no. 11

2. Re-write the above passages as plain harmony by omitting all the embellishing notes.

3. Decorate this piece of harmony with embellishing notes.

4. Harmonise these well-known tunes with chords I, IV and V. Treat the notes between chords as either notes of the same chord or embellishing notes. (Auxiliary notes *above* usually belong to the key; auxiliary notes *below* are often a semitone away and may be outside the key.)

Foster: *The Old Folks at Home*

There is a tavern in the town

4.

Mozart: *The Marriage of Figaro*

5.

5. Write four bars of $\frac{3}{4}$ time using the following chord progression: I, IV, V, I (one chord per bar). Compose a melody to fit the chords, using both accented and unaccented passing notes. Remember to write in the bass notes first.

6. Write four bars of $\frac{4}{4}$ time using the same chord scheme as in question 5, but in a different key. Use one chord per bar, then compose a melody above the chords which uses auxiliary notes and appoggiaturas.

Rhythm in melody

Rhythm is a very important part of melody. The beat is the basis of all rhythm – it is the pulse or heartbeat of music.

Rhythm can mean two different things in music:

1. All those things which go to make up the 'time' of a piece – beats, accents, pulse, metre, bars and so on.

2. A particular pattern of time values, for example:

It is this second meaning of rhythm that we are concerned with in this chapter. Rhythm is the most distinctive feature of many songs and pieces of instrumental music. The first movement of Beethoven's Symphony no. 5 is dominated by a simple rhythm:

The chord of D minor does not make a very interesting melody on its own.

D minor chord

But as soon as rhythm is added, the whole picture changes.

Beethoven: Symphony no. 9 in D minor (1st movement)

Rhythmic plans

There are, of course, hundreds of different rhythmic patterns possible in music. These are some of the more basic ways in which composers over several centuries have used them.

1. Repeated rhythm

The rhythmic pattern is simply repeated.

Dvořák: Wind Serenade, Op. 44

2. Persistent repetition

A rhythmic idea is continually repeated throughout a piece or section of a piece.

Chopin: Prelude in A, Op. 28 no. 7

3. Varied repetition

Repetition can become tedious if continued for too long, but when the repeated rhythm is changed slightly it takes on a new meaning.

Brahms: Violin Concerto in D (2nd movement)

Sometimes a rhythm is repeated once exactly, and then varied.

Couperin: *Soeur Monique* for harpsichord

4. Two rhythms repeated

There are two main ways of using two different rhythms:
1. A, A, B, B.

Musorgsky: *Sorochintsy Fair*

2. A, B, A, B.

Grieg: Piano Concerto in A minor

These four plans:

1. Provide more variety in rhythm.
2. Make longer melodies possible.
3. Give balance to the music.

The four types of rhythmic plan we have already looked at are all well balanced and in equal proportions (symmetrical).

The following types of rhythm are not so regular or balanced (asymmetrical).

5. Metre change

Music in the 15th and 16th centuries often used very free rhythm, without bar lines or regular metre. In order to make the writing of music more clear, bar lines were introduced in the 17th century. Then for nearly three centuries, composers used regular metres with a time signature. The metre remained the same throughout unless a different time signature replaced the original one. In the late 19th century and in the 20th, composers became more interested in using a variety of metres during a piece. They saw no reason why the metre had to stay the same for any length of time.

Vaughan Williams: Love Duet from *Hugh the Drover*

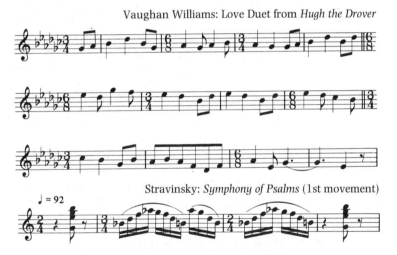

Stravinsky: *Symphony of Psalms* (1st movement)

6. Syncopation

Syncopation is the use of an accent on a beat which is usually weak or unaccented. This is often associated with jazz, but it has also been used in traditional music for hundreds of years. Regular beats may be going on in one part while the other part is syncopated.

Bach: *Two-Part Invention* no. 6

Regular beats: 1   2   3   1   2   3   1   2   3   1

Or the syncopation can be in all parts at the same time. This passage is first heard in syncopated rhythm with accents on the second (weak) beat.

Beethoven: Symphony no. 3 in E flat

Beethoven then repeats it in regular time.

7. Other methods   Melodic movement can also be influenced by quickening the speed and rhythmic values. This melody is repeated 18 times: the interest and excitement increases as the music becomes louder and faster, building up to a grand climax at the end of the piece.

Grieg: 'In the Hall of the Mountain King' from *Peer Gynt*

At the end of his *Magnificat*, Lennox Berkeley lengthens the notes to make a climax. The effect is equally dramatic and exciting.

Berkeley: *Magnificat*

There are many other ways of achieving rhythmic variety. Polyrhythm, for example, uses two different metres in the same phrase at the same time.

Composers in the 20th century have experimented in many ways with this most basic kind of musical movement – rhythm. As you become more involved in composing your own melody and harmony, you may wish to discover more about this fascinating subject.

WORK ON RHYTHM IN MELODY

1. These melodies use one of the rhythmic pattern arrangements. Copy out the melodies, then sing or play through each. State which pattern is used, and mark out details above the stave, as shown in this example.

Example:

Mendelssohn: *Overture: The Hebrides (Fingal's Cave)*

Repeated rhythmic pattern

Mozart: Symphony no. 41 in C ('The Jupiter')

8.

2. Continue each of these given rhythmic ideas in four different ways. Use the rhythmic pattern ideas from question 1.

1.

2.

3.

4.

5.

3. Use these notes to write (a) a syncopated melody, and (b) a melody with metre change.

Harmonising melodies and part-writing

When harmonising melody there is no single solution which is right. The same folk tune has been harmonised by different composers in very different ways. Bach composed many versions of harmony for the same chorale tune. A melody with embellishing notes is more difficult to harmonise than one with just chord notes – there is a wider choice of chords.

Here is a good method to follow:

1. Play or sing the melody several times to discover its style. Is it a slow- or fast-moving melody? What are its dynamics (louds and softs)? Does it move smoothly in a flowing style, or are there slower and longer notes? The speed and style of a melody are important as they will help you to decide how often the harmony needs to change. A simple folk tune will need fewer chords than a hymn tune. Bars 1 and 2 of this folk tune could be harmonised as:

Folk Song: *The Lincolnshire Poacher*

When I was bound— ap - pren - tice

There is nothing wrong with the harmony itself, but to use so many chords in this simple and flowing melody makes the music very crowded. The tempo is too fast for so many chord changes. What this tune really needs is a few chords on the prominent or accented beats, with rests in between.

Folk Song: *The Lincolnshire Poacher*

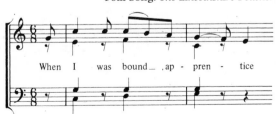

When I was bound— ap - pren - tice

But, in comparison, it would not be suitable to use this simpler style of harmony for a slower-moving chorale tune.

Bach: Cantata no. 65

So, when the melody has longer and slower-moving notes, you will generally use more chords to keep the rhythm going. When the melody notes are short, there will be fewer chords, and the added parts will often be in longer note values.

2. Try to decide which notes in the melody are chord notes and which are embellishing notes.

3. Mark in the cadences and try to vary these as far as the melody will allow.

4. Add the complete bass part.

5. Fill in the inner parts.

Using this plan, let us think about how we would harmonise this melody.

The British Grenadiers

As you play or sing the melody, you will immediately notice that the tune is bright and cheerful, and in a quite fast tempo. We must therefore avoid using too many chords, especially with the semiquaver notes. Treat these as embellishing notes where possible.

The next task is to mark in the cadences. It is necessary to use mainly perfect cadences because of repetition in the tune, but we can obtain some variety with an imperfect cadence at the end of the third phrase.

The British Grenadiers

Embellishing notes and cadences marked in
A = Appoggiatura   P = Passing note   AP = Accented passing note   X = Auxiliary note

We now complete the bass part. Notice that I, IV and V can be used throughout.

The British Grenadiers

All that is left is to fill in the other voices. There are longer notes at the end of phrases 1, 2 and 4, so here is an opportunity to keep the rhythm moving in the bass by using ideas from the melody.

Embellishing notes add interest to music, so look for places where they could be included in the alto and tenor parts. The auxiliary notes at (a) could also be written in the alto a 3rd or 6th from the soprano. The appoggiatura at (b) and the accented passing note at (c) could be doubled in the tenor a 6th below. The unaccented passing note at (d) could be doubled in the alto a 3rd below.

We have now added some interest in the part-writing and can fill in the remaining alto and tenor notes.

The British Grenadiers

It is important now to check the work through and correct any mistakes which may have appeared. Sing or play each of the parts in turn and then play the complete harmonised version.

1. Does the part-writing have any awkward leaps?
2. Are there parallel 5ths or 8ves?
3. Are there exposed 5ths or 8ves?
4. Have we doubled the leading note?
5. Does the leading note move to a note other than the tonic?
6. If there is a unison note in the harmony, do the parts approach or leave it by similar motion?
7. Do the parts overlap or cross?

If your answer to any of these questions is 'Yes', then the part-writing will need to be simplified or changed.

Leading note   The leading note need not move to the tonic if:

1. It is part of a descending scale, 8–7–6.
2. It is in the alto or tenor and the next chord is I. The leading note may then move to the 5th to make a complete chord which would not otherwise have the 5th in it.

Bach: Cantata no. 19

         V   I

3. Chord V is repeated, the leading note may move to another note of the same chord.

4. It falls but rises again to reach the tonic as part of a decorated phrase.

Parallel 5ths and 8ves   Composers of traditional music often avoided these parallel intervals in their music unless a special effect was required. Students of harmony often find this point rather puzzling. Why do text books say that it is wrong to use parallel (or consecutive) 5ths and octaves when some composers use them all the time? The answer is that composers use these parallel sounds mainly in keyboard and instrumental music for special effects such as colouring or emphasising a part. Parallel octaves between the soprano and tenor parts here produce a rich effect.

Beethoven: Piano Sonata in A flat, Op. 26

Parallel 5ths can make music sound rather ancient or primitive.

Vaughan Williams: *Pastoral Symphony*

Our study of harmony is first of all concerned with the choral style – music to be sung. In this type of music, parallel intervals can make the part-writing sound rather weak.

Exposed 5ths and 8ves

An exposed 5th or octave occurs when two parts move in similar motion to the interval of a 5th or octave.

Exposed 8ve   Exposed 5th

As a general rule, try not to use similar motion in the outside parts (S and B) when moving to an octave or 5th. This will make the harmonic movement sound weak especially if the chord changes.

You may use exposed intervals:

1. When the upper part moves by a smaller interval than the lower part.

Haydn: Symphony no. 103 in E flat (4th movement)

2. When there is a move from one position to another of the same chord.

Bach: Chorale *Herr, ich denk an jener Zeit*

**Overlapping
or crossing of
parts**

Although composers often write voice parts which cross or overlap, this needs skilful handling and is best avoided at this stage. It can cause confusion between parts. Bach often crosses the voice parts to keep an interesting melodic shape in one or more of them.

Bach: Chorale *Wachet auf*

* = Alto and tenor cross

You may overlap parts when the same chord changes position.

Handel: *Water Music*

* = Parts overlap

WORK ON HARMONISING MELODIES AND PART-WRITING

1. Copy out these chord progressions. Say whether you think the part-writing is good or weak. Give your reasons.

Example:

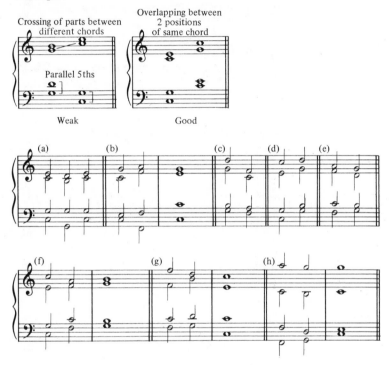

2. Make a list of the weak points in this harmonisation and where each occurs.

3. Harmonise these melodies using primary triads (I, IV and V). Embellishing notes are marked for you in the first two examples. Try to decide which notes embellish the chord notes in examples 3 and 4, and mark these before you start your harmonisation.

German Folk Song: *Fuchs, du hast die Gans gestohlen*

Summary of the weak points in part-writing.

1. Parallel 5ths and 8ves.
2. Exposed 5ths and 8ves.
3. Crossing or overlapping parts.
4. Awkward intervals, e.g. augmented, diminished, 7ths.
5. 3rd omitted.
6. 3rd doubled.
7. Leading note does not rise.
8. Leading note doubled.
9. Notes outside the vocal ranges.
10. Too many leaps in the voice parts.
11. Chords not changing according to the metre.

The motive

A *motive* is a short melodic or rhythmic fragment, usually between one and four bars long. A melody or phrase may have several motives. When we hear a finished melody it is complete in itself – a unified whole. But composers will often start with a few small ideas, and these bits and pieces are the motives of melody. There are many examples of motives in well-known tunes:

Britten: 'Storm' from *4 Sea Interludes from Peter Grimes*

Mendelssohn: *Overture: The Hebrides (Fingal's Cave)*

Spiritual: *When the Saints*

A group of notes is only called a motive when it is repeated exactly or in a slightly altered version (varied).

A motive ends when:

1. It is followed by a rest.

Chopin: Etude in C minor ('The Revolutionary'), Op. 10 no. 12

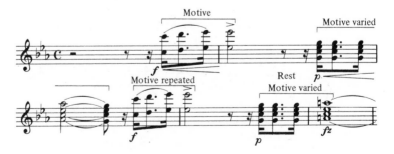

2. It is immediately repeated.

Beethoven: *Overture: Coriolanus*, Op. 62

3. New material is introduced.

Dvořák: *Slavonic Dance* in F, Op. 46 no. 4

In larger works, the repetition of the motive may sometimes be put off until some contrasting material has been heard.

Bizet: Entr'acte from *Carmen*

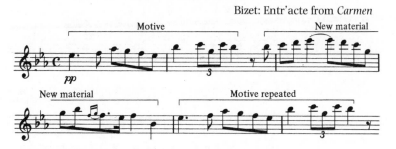

Motives may be:

1. Mainly melodic – a certain interval or shape stands out more than the rhythm.

Bach: Fugue in E from *The Well-Tempered Clavier*, Book II

Russian Folk Song: *Song of the Volga Boatmen*

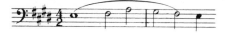

2. Rhythmic – using an interesting rhythm rather than a shapely melody.

Sibelius: *Finlandia*

3. Rhythmic and melodic – this is the most common type, with interesting rhythm, intervals and shape.

Dvořák: Symphony no. 9 in E minor (1st movement)

4. Short and simple.

Beethoven: Symphony no. 5 in C minor

5. Longer and more involved.

Rodrigo: *Concierto de Aranjuez* (3rd movement)

6. Uneven (irregular) in length – this motive is five beats long and does not fit exactly into a bar.

Prokofiev: Violin Concerto no. 2 (1st movement)

WORK ON MOTIVES

1. Copy out these melodies, play or sing them, then:

a) Mark the motive with a bracket

b) Is the repetition exact, varied, or is the motive followed by new material?

c) Say whether the motive is mainly melodic, mainly rhythmic or a mixture of both.

Example:

Handel: Concerto in F (1st movement)

Rimsky-Korsakov: *Scheherezade*, Op. 35 (2nd movement)

Roussel: Symphony no. 3 in G minor (3rd movement)

Wagner: *The Flying Dutchman*

Dvořák: *Slavonic Dance* in E minor, Op. 72 no. 2

Smetana: Polka from *The Bartered Bride*

5.

2. Follow each of these motives with a repetition. You may repeat exactly, vary, invert or extend the motive, but use a variety of treatments.

Example:

Elgar: *Variations on an Original Theme*

Borodin: *Polovtsian Dances*

6.

1-bar motive

J. Strauss: *Tales from the Vienna Woods*

7.

2-bar motive

Brahms: *Hungarian Dance no. 5*

8.

3-bar motive

De Falla: *Ritual Fire Dance*

9.

4-bar motive

Bartók: *Mikrokosmos*, Book IV

10.

5-bar motive

3. Compose four motives of your own of different lengths, then answer each with at least one repetition, either varied or exact.

CHAPTER EIGHT

Secondary triads

Secondary triads are built on the 2nd, 3rd, 6th and 7th degrees of
a scale.

This means that we now have seven chords which correspond to
the seven steps of the scale – a different chord for each note. In
major keys the primary triads (I, IV and V) are always major, and
the secondary triads (II, III and VI) are always minor. VII is a
diminished triad.

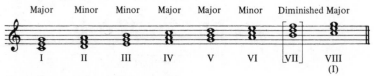

Secondary triads make it possible:

1. To write more varied and interesting harmony, because they can
be used as alternatives to I, IV and V. (Primary triads are still the
strongest way of fixing the key of a piece.)
2. To write smoother and more flowing bass parts.

To make these points clear we shall look at the hymn tune *Old
Hundredth*. It is possible to harmonise this melody with all primary
triads, but the result would be rather dull and lacking variety.

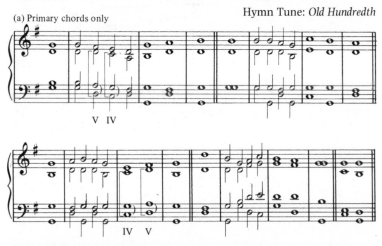

[= Parallel 8ves   ) = Parallel 5ths

But if we replace just a few of the primary triads with secondary
triads you will see what a difference this makes.

Hymn Tune: *Old Hundredth*

(b) Primary and secondary chords

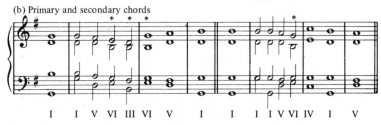

I   I V VI III VI   V   I   I   I I V VI IV   I   V

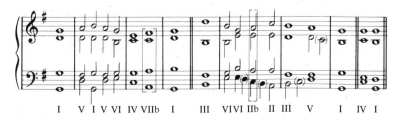

I   V I V VI IV VIIb I   III   VI VI IIb II III   V   I IV I

* = Secondary chord   ( ) = Passing note

The use of secondary triads means that the tonic note can now be
harmonised in three different ways – with chord I, IV or VI.
You can see this most clearly when the tonic is in the soprano part.
In version (a) it is harmonised ten times out of eleven with chord I.
In version (b) three different chords are used for the tonic note – I
six times, VI four times and IV once. This choice of chords gives a
better balance to the music and also helps us overcome certain
problems. It is very difficult not to write parallel 5ths or octaves in
version (a) when the melody and bass are in similar motion. If we
use VI in place of IV in version (b), the outside parts will move in
contrary motion and our problem is solved.

**Secondary
triads as
alternatives**

Each of the secondary triads is closely linked by two common notes
to the primary triad a 3rd above.

Primary and secondary chords with common notes

I   VI   IV   II   V   III

This means that the minor (secondary) triad can be used as an alternative to the major (primary) triad. This is especially useful when:

1. We need to avoid parallel or exposed 5ths and octaves.
2. More varied harmony is needed.

VI in place of I

The last phrase of this well-known carol provides a good example of I being replaced by VI.

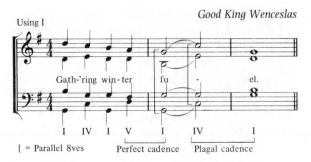

The harmony is weak here because:

1. The tonic chord is used four times out of seven.
2. There are two cadences (perfect then plagal) right at the end. The movement stops too soon at the perfect cadence (V–I), and the final effect of the plagal cadence (IV–I) is spoiled.

This ending to the carol is more interesting and musical.

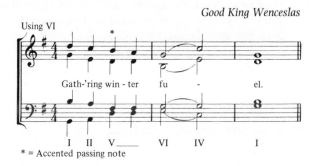

1. VI takes the place of I, and the music now flows through to the final plagal cadence.
2. The use of VI makes a more smooth and flowing bass line.

II in place of IV

Compare these two examples and notice how the first version, using all primary triads, is rather dull.

Campion: *Never weather-beaten sail*

) = Parallel 5ths

The second version has more variety and harmonic movement because II is used in place of IV and VI in place of I.

Campion: *Never weather-beaten sail*

III in place of V

III is often used instead of V when harmonising part of a descending scale. In this example the first three melody notes are 8–7–6, and Brahms uses chords I–III–IV.

Brahms: Symphony no. 4 in E minor (3rd movement)

Chord patterns

The chord pattern I–IV II–V is quite common in music.

Handel: *Water Music*

A descending melody can be harmonised with a falling pattern of chords.

    Melody: 3 falls to 2 falls to 1 falls to 7
    Chords: I falls to V   VI falls to III

Hymn Tune: *St Albinus*

Sometimes the melody demands that we use a secondary triad. There is no alternative to chord II here, as the melody uses all the notes of that chord.

Bach: Little Prelude in F

Notes of chord II
used in harmony as a broken chord

WORK ON SECONDARY TRIADS

1. Write in four parts the secondary triads II, III and VI in each of these keys: D major, F major, A flat major, A major.

Example:

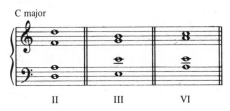

2. Play through this well-known passage, then add chord VI at each * and chord II at †.

3. Copy out this phrase, then add chord symbols (I, II and so on) under the bass line for each chord used. Name and mark the embellishing notes.

Michael Finnigin

4. Play and write out these progressions using a different major key for each:
   II–V–I
   IV–II–V
   I–VI–V–I
   I–III–IV–I
   I–III–VI–IV–II–V–I.

5. Harmonise this descending scale using the suggested mixture of primary/secondary triads. Add a perfect cadence at the end. Continue the falling bass pattern.

I   V   VI   III   IV   I   II   VI   V   I

Transpose this progression into three different major keys. Play through your answers.

6. Harmonise these melodies using both primary and secondary chords.

Mr John Blunt

1.

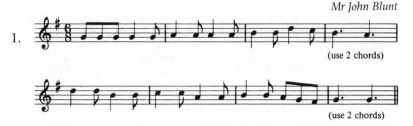

(use 2 chords)

(use 2 chords)

Of all the birds that ever I see

2.

( ) = Embellishing notes

Spanish Ladies

3.

( ) = Embellishing notes

Be careful not to use more than about half secondary chords. You will need to establish the key first by using primary chords, then introduce your secondary chords. End with a perfect cadence.

Motives into melody (1)

There are many ways in which a composer can develop a motive idea into a longer phrase or melody. These are some of the most common methods.

1. Exact repetition

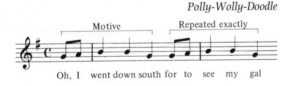

Polly-Wolly-Doodle

2. Sequence

The motive is repeated higher or lower, either:
(a) exactly (a real sequence)

French Round: *Sur le pont d'Avignon*

or (b) varied (a tonal sequence).

Neapolitan Folk Song: *Santa Lucia*

3. Changing intervals

One or more intervals of the motive is changed for variety.

Boëllmann: *Symphonic Variations*

In this example, larger intervals are used each time. This gives the melody a rising shape.

Mozart: Minuet from Serenade in E flat, K375

4. Fragmentation The motive can become rather boring if repeated too often, so composers sometimes repeat only part of it. This is called *fragmentation*.

5. Extension Composers lengthen the motive either by adding a new idea or by using part of it again. This is called *extension*.

6. Inversion Sometimes the motive is turned upside-down (inverted). Exact inversion:

Approximate inversion:

7. Changing the rhythm Shorter time values (diminution):

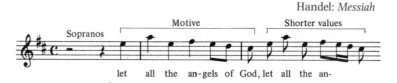

Longer time values (augmentation):

A composer may also move the accent to another note of the motive:

Gershwin: *Fascinating Rhythm*

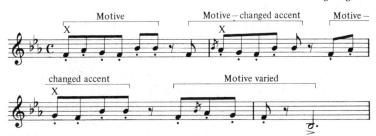

X = Accent (different note each time)

8. Decorated repetition

Composers add embellishing notes (for example, passing notes, appoggiaturas, auxiliary notes, turns) to the motive.

Haydn: Trumpet Concerto (3rd movement)

Composers may use just one or several of these methods when turning a motive into a longer phrase or piece.

This Minuet starts with a two-bar motive.

Purcell: Minuet from Suite no. 1 in G

Purcell develops this short idea into a complete piece by using the motive in a variety of ways:

Bars   1–2   The motive

Bars   3–4   Motive repeated a 4th higher (method 2)

Bars   5–6   The repeated notes of the motive are changed into an interval + two repeated notes, with the rest of the motive moving in the opposite direction (methods 3 and 6)

Bars   7–8   A different interval at the start, then moving by step in the opposite direction with a resting place (cadence) at the end of bar 8 (methods 3, 6 and 7)

Bars   9–10   Upside-down version of motive (method 6)

Bars 11–12   Upside-down version of motive, a 3rd lower than in bars 9–10 (methods 2 and 6)

Bars 13–16   The rising shape of the second part of the motive is repeated three times, each at a lower level, ending with a cadence (methods 4 and 7).

WORK ON MOTIVES INTO MELODY (1)

1. Play through these melodies, then write them out. Mark the motive, then mark and describe the different methods used to vary it in each case.

Example:

Beethoven: *Overture: Fidelio*

Chopin: *Fantaisie* in F minor, Op. 49

1.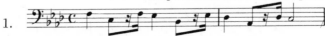

Tchaikovsky: Waltz from *Eugene Onegin*

2.

Mozart: 'Rondo alla turca' from Piano Sonata in A, K331

3.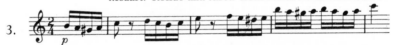

Beethoven: Symphony no. 8 in F (2nd movement)

4.

Bizet: 'La garde montante' from *Carmen*

5.

2. Write eight separate phrases to extend this two-bar motive in different ways. Use the methods described in the previous chapter.

3. Mark and describe the various methods used to develop the motive in this short piece. The music divides into two-bar sections throughout. Use the Minuet by Purcell as your guide.

English Folk Song: *Bobby Shafto*

Movement of chord roots

Music is a language through which the composer speaks to the listener. In this language, chords are the words, and melody the ideas which move us along from one chord to the next. Chords joined together make phrases and sentences. When one chord moves to the next, the bass part can make a strong, medium or weak movement. A building needs a good foundation otherwise it would fall down: we cannot see it but we know it is there. The same is true in music. Many people do not hear movement from the root of one chord to another, but this movement helps to decide the type of music we hear – exciting, strong, flowing or weak.

   This table shows the six common root movements from a bass note; they can be used in any major or minor key. (Roots do not generally move as much as a 7th.)

1. Down a 5th
   (or up a 4th)

2. Down a 4th
   (or up a 5th)

3. Down a 3rd
   (or up a 6th)

4.   Up a 2nd

5. Down a 2nd

6.   Up a 3rd
   (or down a 6th)

In harmony, a rising 4th is the same as a falling 5th, as both go to the same note at a different octave. The same is true of 3rds and 6ths.

Down a 5th (or up a 4th)

This is the strongest and most natural of all root movements. V–I is the foundation of the perfect cadence, but other falling 5ths are almost as strong.

   A sequence of falling 5ths makes the strongest possible progression of chords.

You will find many examples of this pattern in traditional music. Often just part of the pattern is used:

Bach: Chorale *Mit Fried' und Freud'*

Down a 4th (or up a 5th)

Falling 4ths in the bass are also common and make strong movements.

Morley: *Nolo mortem peccatoris*

They are often used together with falling 5ths:

Chopin: Nocturne in G minor, Op. 37 no. 1

Down a 3rd (or up a 6th)

The next strongest root movement is a sequence of falling 3rds.

Wagner: *Parsifal* ('Grail' motive)

One exception is V–III–I, which can sound rather weak because III breaks up the stronger progression of V–I.

Up a 2nd

A bass line of rising 2nds is best when moving from IV–V, V–VI or VII–I.

Gluck: March from *Alceste*

V–VI is often used as an interrupted cadence. The effect is not so final as a perfect or plagal cadence.

Down a 2nd

When the bass falls in 2nds the general effect is usually gentle.

Tchaikovsky: *Fantasy-Overture: Romeo and Juliet*

An exception is the root movement VI–V, which is stronger.

Bach: Chorale *Lob sei dem allmächtigen Gott*

Roots rising or falling a 2nd are often difficult to write because they can easily produce parallel 5ths or octaves.

Up a 3rd (or down a 6th)

I–III–IV makes strong harmonic movement.

Bach: Chorale *Herr Gott dich loben*

( ) = Passing note

Used in any other way, the rising 3rd can sound weak.

You have discovered the importance of hearing and writing melodies in phrases. A melody should not be thought of as individual notes but as an overall shape. The same is true of harmony. Up to now, we have mainly thought of harmony as individual chords, each with a label. From now on, look for shapes in your bass parts as well as in melody.

This table shows all the possible root movements from any one bass note. Each move is graded strong, medium, gentle or weak.

Strong	*Medium*	*Gentle*	*Weak*
Down a 5th (or up a 4th)	Up a 2nd to II, III or IV	Up a 3rd (not I–III–IV)	Up 2 or more 3rds
Down a 4th (or up a 5th)	Down a 2nd to IV, III or I	Down a 2nd III–II	
Down a 3rd (or up a 6th)		Up a 2nd II–III	
Down a 2nd to V			
Up a 2nd to V, VI or I			
Up a 3rd I–III–IV only			

WORK ON ROOT MOVEMENTS

1. Play through and copy out these chord progressions, then:
a) Describe the root movements as strong, medium, gentle or weak
b) Add a symbol for each movement
c) Name each chord
d) Which note is doubled?

Example:

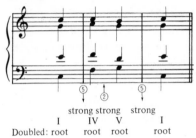

strong strong   strong
    I   IV   V   I
Doubled: root   root root   root

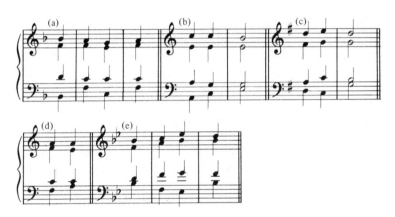

2. Play through and copy out these phrases, then:
a) Name the chords you would use
b) Analyse the root movements and add a symbol for each
c) Complete the alto and tenor parts.

3. Add parts for alto, tenor and bass to these melodies. Use only strong or medium root movements.

4. Write eight bars of your own chord progressions in $\frac{2}{4}$ time in F major. Play your answer through and make any necessary alterations. Then write two more series of progressions in different major keys.

Helpful hints:

1. Start with I and end with a perfect cadence.

2. Use only strong, medium, and the occasional gentle root movements.

3. Use only block chords – two for each bar.

4. Don't use the same chord twice together.

5. If the bass has several leaps the other parts should move by step. If the bass moves by step the soprano may leap.

6. Aim for a good shape in both the soprano and bass parts. It is best to write the bass first, followed by the soprano, then alto and tenor.

7. Use a good variety of chords, including both primary and secondary.

8. Chords should move smoothly onwards to the final cadence.

9. Check your harmony for parallels, overlapping, awkward leaps etc.

Motives into melody (2)

You have looked at eight of the ways in which a composer can develop a motive into a longer phrase or melody. It is important to remember that composers often use a combination of two or more of these methods in the same melody.

Here are five further methods used by composers which rely on repetition of the motive in some form.

1. Changing the order of notes

Musorgsky: *Pictures at an Exhibition*

2. Expansion

The composer adds to the length of the motive by using a new idea. This is much the same as extending the motive, except that the new idea comes in the middle of the motive rather than at the end.

Walton: 'Yodelling Song' from *Façade Suite* no. 1

3. Contraction

The composer shortens the motive by leaving out a small section of it when it is repeated.

Brahms: Violin Concerto in D

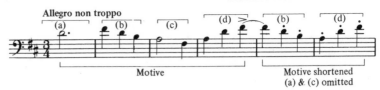

4. Simplifying

The length of the motive stays the same, but some notes are taken out to make a version with less detail.

Verdi: *Requiem*

5. Retrograde
motion

The motive is written backwards. In this example, the two
parts are completely reversible. The lower part is the same as the
upper part when played backwards. The upper part is the same as
the lower part when played backwards.

J.A. André: *Lehrbuch der Tonsetzkunst* (1832–43)

WORK ON MOTIVES INTO MELODY (2)

1. Play through these melodies, then write them out. Mark the motive, then mark and describe the different methods used to vary it in each case.

Example:

Bernstein: 'Maria' from *West Side Story*

Ma - ri - a!_____ I've just met a girl named Ma - ri - a _____

Holst: 'Mars' from *The Planets*

Crotch: Chant in G

(Compare 1 with 3, then 2 with 4)

Rimsky-Korsakov: 'Dance of the Tumblers' from *The Snow Maiden*

Elgar: *Variations on an Original Theme*

Sousa: *March: Semper fidelis*

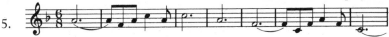

2. Extend this motive by:
a) Changing the order of notes or groups of notes
b) Shortening the motive
c) Expanding the motive
d) Simplifying the motive
e) Writing the motive backwards.

3. Extend these motives by using a combination of two or more of the methods described in Chapters 8 and 9.

6.

7.

8.

First-inversion chords

The triads we have looked at so far have all been in *root position*, that is, with the root of the chord in the bass.

A triad may also have one of its other notes in the bass. When this happens the triad is known as an *inversion*. To make a *first inversion* we simply change the order or position of the notes so that the 3rd of the chord becomes the bass note. The root moves up an octave.

Root position   1st inversion

You will notice that the intervals of a triad in first inversion are a 6th and a 3rd from the bass. For this reason a first inversion is often called a $\frac{6}{3}$ chord, usually shortened to 6.

First inversions are useful for several reasons:

1. To provide more variety in the harmony.
2. To make smoother and more flowing bass lines.
3. Bass lines can have better shapes.
4. More gentle progressions are possible.

Where to use 1st inversions

1. In place of a root position

The first inversion is often used instead of a root position of the same chord. The melody below could be harmonised with three root-position tonic chords at (a) and three root-position dominant chords at (b). Handel prefers, however, to vary the harmony by moving to a $\frac{6}{3}$ chord and then back to its root position. This is good for three reasons.

1. The harmony is more interesting and varied.
2. The bass has a better shape.
3. The accompaniment is in the same light dance style as the melody.

Handel: *Water Music*

<table>
<tr><td>I</td><td>I I⁶ I   V</td><td>V V⁶ V   I</td></tr>
</table>

I   I I⁶ I   V   V V⁶ V   I

2. Parallel 1st inversions

Play through this example and you will hear how parallel 6 chords help to join the harmonies together in a flowing line. This movement is rather like the 'wave' shape in melody.

Handel: 'Oh, never bow we down' from *Judas Maccabaeus*

VI⁶ V⁶ IV⁶III⁶ IV⁶ III⁶   II⁶ I⁶ II⁶ VII⁶

When parallel 6 chords are used in four-part writing it is often difficult to avoid writing parallel 5ths and octaves. To overcome this problem, one of the parts must not move parallel with the other three.

In this example, the soprano, alto and bass move in parallel, but the tenor does not move in the same direction – it jumps about. In this way, Mozart avoids writing parallel 5ths or octaves.

Mozart: March from *The Magic Flute*

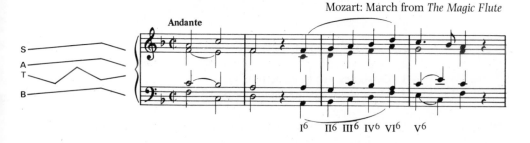

I⁶   II⁶ III⁶ IV⁶ VI⁶   V⁶

3. VII⁶ as a passing chord

The diminished triad VII is used more in its first-inversion form than in root position. VII⁶ is often used as a passing chord between I and I⁶, or I⁶ and I.

Note:

1. All voice parts move by step.

2. Outside voice parts move in contrary motion.

3. The bass note (the 3rd of VII) is doubled in VII^6.

4. The parallel 5ths between alto and tenor are permissible because the 5th in VII is diminished while the 5th in I is perfect. The primitive sound of parallel perfect 5ths is avoided.

This example shows another way of arranging the voice parts in this progression.

Mendelssohn: *St Paul*

4. V^6 and I^6 as auxiliary chords

An auxiliary note in melody moves one step up or down, then returns to the original note. An auxiliary chord is much the same – three of the voices move to the next note up or down while the fourth voice stays on the same note.

In this example, V^6 appears between two root positions of the tonic chord and I^6 between two root positions of the subdominant chord.

5. 1st inversions leading to a cadence

A rising or falling bass line of first-inversion chords often makes a good lead up to a perfect or imperfect cadence.

Purcell: *Dido and Aeneas*

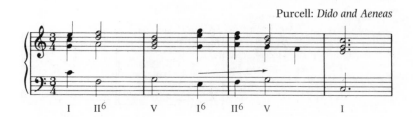

I   II⁶   V   I⁶   II⁶   V   I

Purcell: *Come, ye sons of art*

I   V⁶   IV⁶   V   II⁶   I⁶   IV   (V⁷)   I

Purcell: Suite no. 4 in A minor

A minor
II⁶   I⁶   VII⁶   I   V⁶   IV⁶   V

Imperfect cadence

**Points
to remember**

When you write ⁶₃ chords it is generally better to double the root or the 5th.

1. Doubling

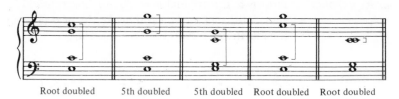

Root doubled   5th doubled   5th doubled   Root doubled   Root doubled

The 3rd may be doubled:

a) When the outer parts move by step in contrary motion.

3rd doubled

b) In a minor triad.

3rd doubled   3rd doubled

c) In the first inversion of a diminished triad.

Diminished triad (VII⁶)

3rd doubled

2. Movement of bass parts

Root and bass are no longer the same. Root movements are determined by the chord and not by the bass note. First inversions can be used by step for a flowing phrase. This would not be possible using root positions.

I⁶   II⁶   II⁶   IV⁶   V⁶   VI⁶   VII⁶   I⁶

3. Mixing chords

Root positions and first inversions are often mixed together for contrasts of strong and gentle movement.

Lawes: *Farley Castle*

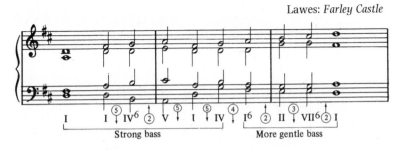

I   I   IV⁶   V   I   IV   I⁶   II   VII⁶   I

Strong bass   More gentle bass

4. Bass notes

The bass note in a first inversion is no longer the root of the chord.

WORK ON FIRST-INVERSION CHORDS

1. Harmonise these bass notes in four parts as first inversions of primary triads. Write four different arrangements and label each chord.

Example:

I⁶

2. Harmonise these melody notes in four parts as first inversions of secondary triads. Write the 3rd of the chord as the bass note, then add the other parts.

Example:

II⁶

3. Harmonise the following pairs of notes for SATB. Use a root position and a first inversion of the same chord for each.

Example:

I   I⁶

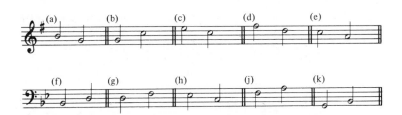

4. Play these two harmonisations of the same melody, then compare them. How are the versions different? Which, in your opinion, is better and why?

5. Harmonise these well-known tunes for SATB. There are some suggestions for the use of first inversions, but include others where appropriate. Use a mixture of primary and secondary triads. You now have more chords to choose from, so there may be several possible ways of harmonising a phrase. Look for places where you can use the progressions you have learnt. Remember that it is important for both the melody and bass to have a good shape and flow.

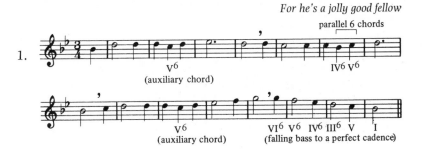

For he's a jolly good fellow

Irish Folk Song: *St Patrick was a gentleman*
parallel 6 chords

I⁶   VII⁶   VI⁶   V⁶   IV⁶

Use 2 chords per bar

Student Song: *Gaudeamus igitur*

Mostly 2 or 3 chords per bar

Phrase structure (1)

You have looked at many of the musical ingredients used by composers when writing melody – intervals, melodic shape, unity of style, climax and rest, rhythm and metre, the motive, and different ways of treating the motive.

It is important now to see how composers use these different ideas when arranging and constructing their phrases. There are four methods a composer may use.

1. Motive and variations

This type of melody has been in use from early times to the present day.

Bach: *Two-Part Invention* no. 1

Dvořák: Symphony no. 9 in E minor

2. Motive, variations and new idea

The composer starts with the motive, varies it in some way, then introduces a new idea near the end of the phrase.

Handel: Air from *The Triumph of Time and Truth*

* = Interval change

Bizet: *Carmen*

3. Two motives and variations

This arrangement of ideas provides a good balance and contrast. The first motive is often repeated before the second motive is introduced.

Bach: *Sheep may safely graze*

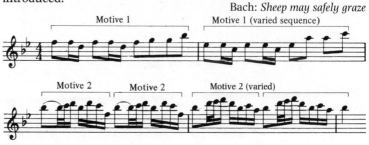

Tchaikovsky: Symphony no. 5 in E minor

4. Free-flowing melody, no repetition

There are many examples of this type of melody or phrase.

Ockeghem: 'Sanctus' from *Missa prolationum*

Beethoven: Symphony no. 4 in B flat (2nd movement)

Perhaps the largest number of examples can be found in music from the Middle Ages and the 20th century.

WORK ON PHRASE STRUCTURE (1)

1. Play through these melodies several times, then analyse the structure of each. Identify the motive, then comment on the way it is developed.

Example:

Mozart: Symphony no. 29 in A

This melody consists of one motive and its variations. These take the form of sequences. The motive is arch-shaped, and the melody uses a wide range of notes.

Lerner and Loewe: 'Get me to the church on time' from *My Fair Lady*

1.

Tchaikovsky: March from *Nutcracker Suite*

2. **Tempo di marcia**

Mendelssohn: *Children's Piece*

3. **Allegro non troppo**

Bernstein: 'America' from *West Side Story*

Walton: *Coronation March: Crown Imperial*

2. Write three melodies of eight bars each. Use the following plans:

Melody 1: a motive and its variations
Melody 2: a motive and its variations, then new material
Melody 3: two motives with variations on each of them.

You may use these motives or make up your own. Remember to include some of these ideas: repetition, inversion, sequence, interval changes, augmentation, diminution.

Holst: 'Dargason' from *St Paul's Suite*

Handel: 'The Trumpet shall Sound' from *Messiah*

Vaughan Williams: March from *Folk Song Suite*
Melody 3 (Motive 1)

Melody 3 (Motive 2)

3. Compose a flowing melody of eight bars with no repetition of ideas.

Second-inversion chords

A second-inversion triad is formed by moving the root and 3rd above the 5th of a root-position triad.

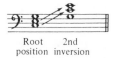

Root   2nd
position inversion

The 5th becomes the bass of the chord. The intervals of a second-inversion triad are a 6th and a 4th from the bass note. This is why the second inversion is called a $^6_4$ chord.

Second inversions may be built up on all steps of the scale.

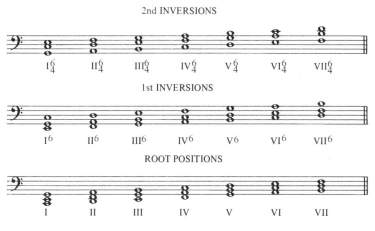

Second inversions were used long before 18th-century writers on harmony gave them their name. The chord was often heard as two embellishing notes sounded together when passing from one chord to another.

Purcell: *Almand*

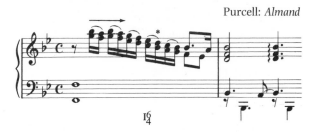

Main uses of the $\frac{6}{4}$

1. Cadential $\frac{6}{4}$

This use of the $\frac{6}{4}$ comes so often at cadence points and this is why it is called 'cadential'. It precedes V and is used to 'decorate' it.

(a) Perfect cadence   Becomes:

VI   V   I   VI   I$\frac{6}{4}$ V   I

Bass doubled

(b) Interrupted (or perfect) cadence   Becomes:

II^6 V   VI (or) I   II^6 I$\frac{6}{4}$ V   VI (or) I

Bass doubled

(c) Imperfect cadence   Becomes:

II   V   II   I$\frac{6}{4}$ V

Bass doubled

Note:

1. The $\frac{6}{4}$ chord comes on an accented beat.

2. The bass note of a $\frac{6}{4}$ chord is always doubled – the 4th and 6th are used only once each.

3. The bass note and one other stay the same, while the other two parts resolve (usually by step) on to V.

Cadential $^6_4$ to a perfect cadence:

D major
* = Double appoggiatura

         II^6 I$^6_4$ V   I

Cadential $^6_4$ to an imperfect cadence:

Mendelssohn: Symphony no. 3 in A minor

C major   II^6 I$^6_4$ V
* = Double appoggiatura

2. Passing $^6_4$ The $^6_4$ is often used when passing between one chord and another.

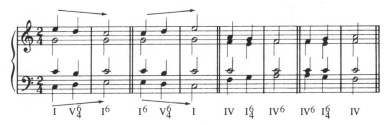

I   V$^6_4$ I^6 I^6 V$^6_4$ I   IV   I$^6_4$ IV^6 IV^6 I$^6_4$ IV

Note:

1. The bass moves up or down three steps and one of the other parts does the same thing in contrary motion.

2. A third part stays on the same note, which is common to all three chords.

3. The passing $^6_4$ moves to and from the main harmony and so appears on a weak beat.

4. The passing $^6_4$ links a root-position chord and its first inversion, or vice versa.

Gluck: March from *Alceste*

D major   I   V⁶₄   I⁶

3. Auxiliary ⁶₄

Two voice parts move up by step, then back again, while the other two parts remain on the same note. The ⁶₄ usually comes on a weak beat.

I   IV⁶₄   I   V   I⁶₄   V   II   V⁶₄   II

This use of the second inversion can be seen in this well-known piece.

Brahms: *Variations on a Theme of Haydn*

I   IV⁶₄ I

4. Arpeggio ⁶₄

If the bass moves up or down as a broken chord, a ⁶₄ occurs before the music reaches a root position again.

Salieri: March from *Palmira*

I   I   I⁶   I⁶₄   I   I   I   I⁶   I⁶₄   I

This bass movement is more suitable for instrumental than choral writing.

WORK ON SECOND-INVERSION CHORDS

1. Harmonise these bass notes as second inversions. Write three different arrangements and label each chord. Always double the bass note.

Example:

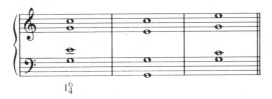

2. Play through these extracts, then describe how the $^6_4$ chords are used in each case.

J.N. Bach

Silent Night

Si - lent night, ho - ly night

Mozart: Piano Sonata in A, K331

Meyerbeer: *Coronation March*

Hymn Tune: *Richmond*

3. Write a cadential $^6_4$ leading to:

a) a perfect cadence in D major

b) an imperfect cadence in F major

c) an interrupted cadence in B flat major.

Example:

Perfect cadence

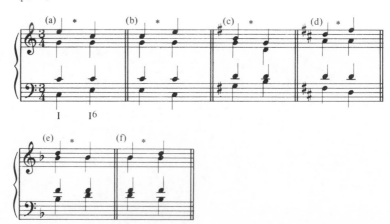

4. Add the appropriate second inversion to make these passing $^6_4$ progressions.

5. Harmonise the following as auxiliary $\substack{6 \\ 4}$ progressions.

6. Harmonise these melodies for SATB. Use $\substack{6 \\ 4}$ chords where indicated.

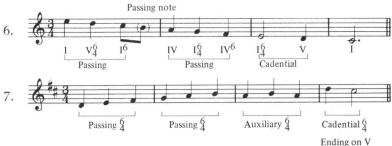

7. Harmonise these melodies for SATB. Use a selection of root position, $\substack{6 \\ 3}$ and $\substack{6 \\ 4}$ primary and secondary chords.

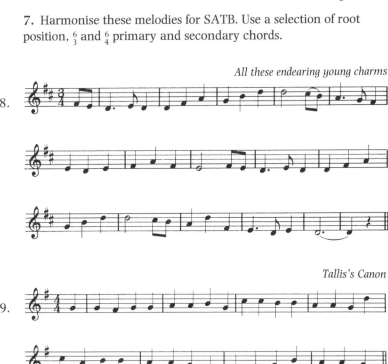

The Lorelei

10.

Hymn Tune: Hursley

11.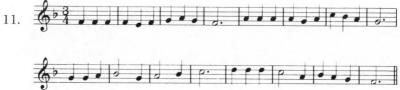

Phrase structure (2)

There is no rule to say how long a phrase should be. Phrases may be regular (2, 4, 8 bars) or irregular (3, 5, 7 bars, or even without bars).

Regular phrases

When one phrase exactly equals another in length (for example, 4 bars + 4 bars) it is called symmetrical. Music and dance have always been closely linked, and symmetrical music probably began as a result of dance patterns. Regular patterns of dance steps would need regular patterns of music. So we find many popular and dance tunes with symmetrical phrases, even though composers may use irregular phrase lengths in their own music.

Estampie (13th-century instrumental dance)

From the middle of the 18th century, well-balanced phrase patterns became the order of the day. You will find examples of symmetrical phrases in nearly all Classical and Romantic music. The four-bar phrase was the most common in the Classical period.

Mozart: Piano Sonata in A, K331

Irregular phrases

Phrases of course do not have to be four or eight bars long, and composers have often welcomed the chance to use irregular phrases. This helps to break up what could become a rather mechanical plan. Here are some examples:

Three-bar phrases

Brahms: *The Nightingale*

Five-bar phrase

Haydn: String Quartet in F minor, Op. 20 no. 5

Phrase without bar lines or metre

Puccini: Recitative from *La bohème* (Act I)

Repeating the phrase

A motive is a musical fragment which, when repeated in some way, forms a phrase or melody. A phrase may also be repeated in a number of different ways, but it is best to keep the general shape and final cadence the same.

1. By repeating exactly – either by using repeat marks and a double bar, or by writing it out twice.

Flotow: 'The Last Rose of Summer' from *Martha*

2. By making the melody more elaborate.

Chopin: Nocturne in E flat, Op. 9 no. 2

4-bar phrase

Andante

4-bar phrase with variations

3. By changing the register (for example, writing the phrase an octave higher).

Handel: 'Awful pleasing being, say' from *Joshua*

Largo   2-bar phrase   Octave higher

4. By changing the style of accompaniment.

Sweelinck: *Est-ce Mars*

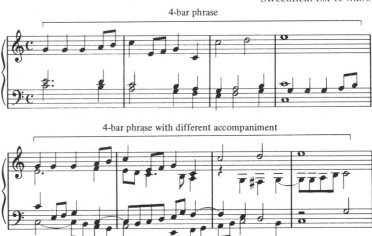

4-bar phrase

4-bar phrase with different accompaniment

WORK ON PHRASE STRUCTURE (2)

1. Play through these melodies, then:
a) Number the bars
b) Add phrase marks and give details of phrase lengths
c) Say whether the phrases are symmetrical or irregular
d) Say how the phrase is repeated.

Example:

Brahms: Piano Trio in C minor, Op. 101

This melody has two regular 4-bar phrases and is symmetrical

Beethoven: *Overture: Leonora no. 3*

1.

Plainchant: Offertory *Afferentur regi virgines* (Mode IV)

2.

Tu es   pa-stor o - vi - um prin - ceps A - po - sto - lo - rum
(Thou art the shepherd of the sheep, the Prince of the Apostles)

Edwardes: *When May is in his prime*

3.

May makes the cheer-ful   hue,   May breeds and brings new blood

Bizet: Intermezzo 'Les dragons d'Alcala' from *Carmen*

4.

Bach: *Chromatic Fantasy and Fugue*

5.

Bizet: Carillon from *L'Arlésienne Suite* no. 1

2. Compose the following in any major key:

a) Two four-bar balancing phrases (symmetrical)

b) Two irregular phrases (three or five bars each)

c) A phrase in free form without bar lines or metre

d) A phrase repeated exactly

e) A phrase repeated but also varied in some way (for example, decorated version or register change).

CHAPTER TWELVE

Minor harmony

Minor scales

The major scale has only one form, but there are two types of minor scale in common use today: harmonic and melodic.

A scale has eight notes and these notes are divided into two tetrachords (*tetra* is a Greek word which means 'four'). The harmonic and melodic minor scales have the same four notes for the lower tetrachord, but the upper tetrachord of each is different.

HARMONIC MINOR

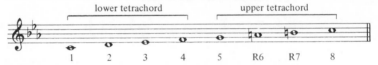

MELODIC MINOR (ascending)

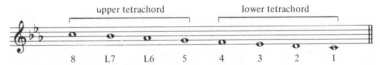

MELODIC MINOR (descending)

R = raised   L = lowered

As a general rule, the harmonic minor scale is the one most used in minor harmony. The melodic minor scale is mainly used to avoid awkward intervals in melody. Both scales have a raised leading note which makes strong movement in cadences.

Harmonic minor   Melodic minor

The main difference between these two minor scales is in their 6th and 7th notes. How do we decide which version to use and when?

1. When 6 moves to 7, both notes are raised (i.e. melodic minor scale ascending).

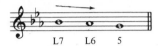

2. When 7 moves to 6, both notes are lowered (i.e. melodic minor scale descending).

Notice how both notes change together when the melody changes direction.

Beethoven: String Quartet in F minor, Op. 95

3. When 6 and 7 are away from each other, 7 is raised and 6 is lowered (i.e. harmonic minor scale).

Bach: Fugue in F minor from *The Well-Tempered Clavier*, Book II

Play or sing this example and notice how 7 seems to want to move up to 8 and how 6 pulls down to 5.

Triads in minor harmony

You are already familiar with major and minor triads, but there are two further types: diminished and augmented. A diminished triad has two minor 3rds stacked on top of each other. An augmented triad has two major 3rds stacked on top of each other.

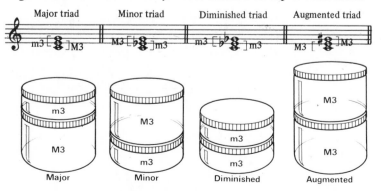

Major and minor triads are consonant (C). Diminished and augmented triads are dissonant (D). Here is a table of the raised and lowered triads as they appear in a minor scale.

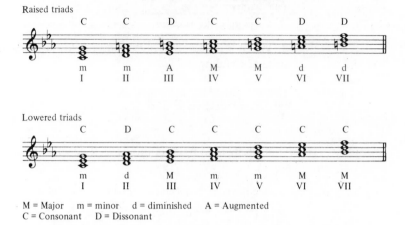

M = Major   m = minor   d = diminished   A = Augmented
C = Consonant   D = Dissonant

Harmony in minor keys will match the movement of the melody.

1. When 6 and 7 are raised we use raised chords.

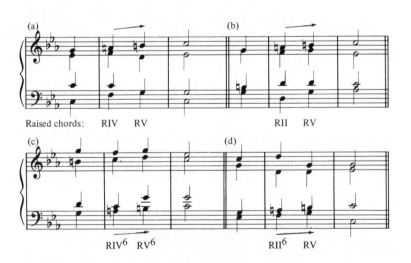

2. When 7 and 6 are lowered we use lowered chords.

C minor

L7　　L6

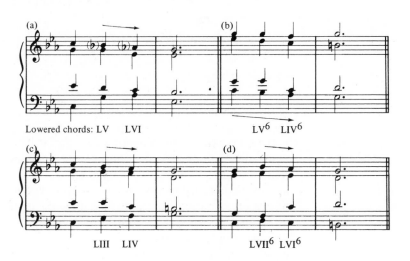

Lowered chords: LV　LVI　　　　LV⁶　LIV⁶

LIII　LIV　　　　LVII⁶ LVI⁶

The series of raised chords is often bright and active.

Gibbons: Song no. 20

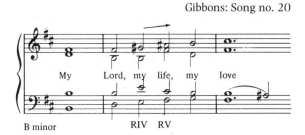

My　　Lord, my　life,　my　　love

B minor　　　　RIV　RV

The lowered chords have no leading note, and their movement is more gentle and dark.

Handel: *Cannons*

F minor LV⁶　LVI⁶　LV⁶　LIV⁶　LIII⁶　LII⁶　LIV⁶

In the melodic minor, chords are usually separated into raised or lowered forms, as you have seen. In the harmonic minor, the two forms are often mixed together. This makes a contrast between brightness and darkness in the same phrase.

Bach: Sarabande from English Suite no. 2

A minor   LII⁶   RV LVI   RV

Minor triads in root position, first and second inversion, serve much the same purpose as major triads.

Here is a hymn tune in a minor key. You will notice that many of the ideas you have used in major harmony work just as well in minor harmony. There are examples of:

a) strong and solid movement of root-position chords
b) variety of harmony, smooth bass lines and gentle progressions as a result of first-inversion chords
c) a passing $^6_4$ in the minor
d) a cadential $^6_4$ in the minor

Embellishing notes (those of a semitone are more forceful than those of a tone):

e) single and double passing notes
f) anticipation
g) auxiliary notes
h) perfect and imperfect cadences (all four cadences are used in minor keys as in major keys).

J. Parry: *Aberystwyth*

(e)   (a) (a) (a) (a)   (a)   (a) (a)

(e)

(g)

(b) (b) (b)

(b)

Dissonant triads in minor harmony

There are three diminished triads and one augmented triad in all minor keys.

	Diminished	Diminished	Diminished	Augmented
	dII(L)	dVI(R)	dVII(R)	AIII(R)

L = lowered   R = raised

The 5th note of all these triads is an unstable note. For this reason it needs to be prepared (sounded) in the same voice part of the previous chord. In diminished chords the 5th then moves down by step. In augmented chords the 5th then moves up by step.

dII   dVI   dVII   AIII

P = prepared

1. Diminished triads

Diminished triads are used more in first inversion than in root position. II⁶ is often heard as part of a cadence.

Beethoven: Piano Sonata in G minor, Op. 49 no. 1

G minor   II⁶   I⁶₄   V

VII⁶ is seen here moving to I.

Handel: *Messiah*

D minor   VII⁶

But VII⁶ is used mainly as a passing or auxiliary chord.

Mendelssohn: *St Paul*

D minor   I⁶ VII⁶ I   I⁶ VII⁶ I

2. Augmented triad

The augmented triad (III) resolves on to VI, as shown on p. 149. III⁶ with the root in the top voice is sometimes used in place of V in a perfect or interrupted cadence. The 5th in this case need not be prepared.

Purcell: *The Fairy Queen*

G minor   III⁶

Once you have understood how to use the raised and lowered forms of minor keys, you should have no trouble completing the harmony for a minor melody.

Tierce de Picardie

Before the 16th century a final chord often had no 3rd. After this time you will sometimes find that the last chord in a minor-key piece has a major 3rd rather than a minor 3rd. This is known as the *tierce de picardie* (or 'Picardy 3rd').

Farmer: Psalm 146

A minor

Major 3rd
Tierce de Picardie

WORK ON MINOR HARMONY

1. Write the following minor scales with key signatures, ascending and descending, in both harmonic and melodic forms: B minor, G minor, F minor, A minor, F sharp minor.

2. Write perfect, imperfect, plagal and interrupted cadences in: G minor, B minor, C minor. The 3rd should be doubled in VI as part of the interrupted cadence.

3. Write out the raised and lowered forms of the triads as they appear in: A minor, D minor, E minor, F minor.
Mark each triad as consonant (C) or dissonant (D). Say whether the triad is major (M), minor (m), diminished (d) or augmented (A).

4. Insert raised or lowered chords where indicated in these progressions. Play your answers, then transpose them into three different minor keys.

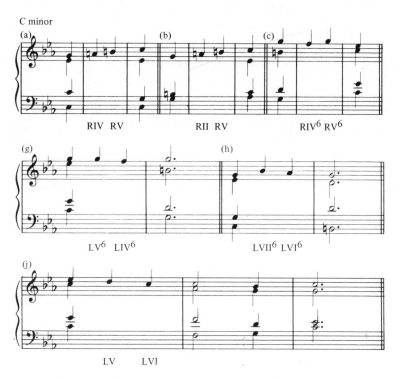

5. Harmonise these fragments using raised and lowered root positions and first inversions where appropriate.

6. Write one chord either side of these augmented and diminished chords to prepare and resolve them.

Example:

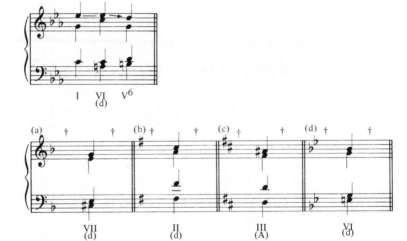

† = insert chord

7. Write chord progressions to illustrate:

a) II⁶ as part of a cadence: I II⁶ I$^6_4$ V VI in D minor

b) VII⁶ as a passing chord: I V⁶ I VII⁶ I⁶ I$^6_4$ V I in B minor

c) VII⁶ as an auxiliary chord: I VII⁶ I V⁶ in G minor.

8. Harmonise these minor melodies.

Traditional Carol: *The Bellman's Song*

Bach: *St John Passion*

2.

Folk Song: *The Miller of the Dee*

3.

Coventry Carol

4.

Tierce de Picardie

Minor melody

People often think that music in minor keys is sad, but this is far
from the truth. The two versions of the minor scale offer us a good
choice in our melody writing. They can, of course, be sad:

but they can be lively as well:

Harmonic minor melody

It is best to avoid using the augmented intervals of this scale in
your melody writing for the time being. If, for any reason, you
decide to use this scale, the best way to avoid the augmented
intervals is to invert them so that they become diminished.
(An augmented interval is one semitone larger than perfect or major;
a diminished interval is one semitone smaller than perfect or minor.)

When you have inverted the augmented intervals, follow two simple
rules:

1. Go to the leading note from above, or from note 5.
2. The note after the diminished interval should be inside the leap.

Beethoven: Piano Concerto no. 3 in C minor

Bach: Fugue in F minor from *The Well-Tempered Clavier*, Book II

Melodic minor melody

Melodies using both the lowered and raised forms of this scale can be colourful and dramatic. It is a good idea to approach and leave notes 6 and 7 by step.

Vivaldi: Violin Concerto in A minor

Mixing harmonic and melodic minor melody

Sometimes both harmonic and melodic forms of the minor scale are mixed together in melody. It is important to remember that they are different forms of the same scale, not two different scales. They can work quite happily together if handled carefully.

Bach: Prelude in A minor from *The Well-Tempered Clavier*, Book II

Unusual patterns

Occasionally the raised form of the melodic minor may be used in a descending pattern of notes, or the lowered form in an ascending pattern. This is just the opposite of the general rule, but it sometimes occurs.

The raised form of 6 and 7 can be used in a falling melody when the chord used with or suggested by the melody is V.

Loeillet: Gigue from Suite in G minor

The lowered 6th may rise when the melodic pattern is 6–7–6–5.

Grieg: Piano Concerto in A minor

Raised and lowered forms of the same note are sometimes heard at the same time. This is known as a *false relation*.

Haydn: String Quartet in D, Op. 71 no. 2

Composers use this idea only for special dramatic effects, and you would be wise to avoid it at present.

WORK ON MINOR MELODY

1. Play through these minor melodies, then say whether the harmonic or melodic form is used or a mixture of both. Mark details on your copy of the music where the different forms occur.

Example:

Scarlatti: Sonata in D minor

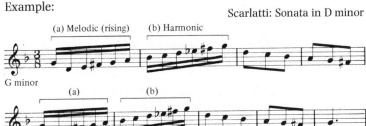

This melody uses a mixture of the harmonic and ascending melodic forms of G minor.

Berlioz: *Rákóczy March*

Beethoven: Piano Sonata in C sharp minor, Op. 27 no. 2

Dukas: *The Sorcerer's Apprentice*

Mozart: *Requiem*

Beethoven: String Quartet in F minor, Op. 95

Tchaikovsky: Symphony no. 4 in F minor

2. Compose two melodies of eight bars each. Use only notes from the harmonic minor scale. You may use the suggested openings, or make up your own.

8.

3. Compose a melody of twelve bars using the melodic form of the minor scale. A motive idea is suggested, or you may choose one of your own.

4. Compose a melody of sixteen bars using a mixture of the harmonic and melodic minor scales in a key of your choice. Use repetition in a fairly simple style and try for a good melodic shape.

The dominant seventh

The dominant 7th (V⁷) has four different notes. It consists of the dominant triad plus a minor 3rd. This extra 3rd forms the interval of a 7th from the root of the chord, hence the name dominant 7th.

$$V + m3 = V^7$$

V⁷ is the same in both major and minor keys. It has two dissonant intervals.

Minor 7th   Diminished 5th
                 (diabolus in musica)

These dissonant intervals clash and so need to resolve. The 7th of the chord falls by step, and the 3rd rises by a semitone to the tonic.

This means that V⁷ usually moves to chord I or VI.

V⁷ – I   V⁷ – I   V⁷ – I   V⁷ – VI

(♭ = Minor-scale notes)

Uses of V⁷

V⁷ can generally be used as an alternative to V if it is possible to resolve the chord. Here are some examples:

1. V⁷ in a perfect cadence.

Beethoven: Piano Sonata in A flat, Op. 26

Andante

I⁶₄   V⁷   I

2. V⁷ in an interrupted cadence.

Mozart: *The Magic Flute*

I   V⁷   VI

(Notice the doubled 3rd in VI)

3. V⁷ as a richer chord than V.

Haydn: String Quartet in C, Op. 76 no. 3

V (without 7th)   I   V⁷   I

4. V⁷ suggested or outlined by the melody.

Mozart: Piano Sonata in B flat, K333

V⁷   I   V⁷   I

Movement to the 7th of V⁷

1. Movement by step.

Bach: Chorale *Jesu meine Freude*

V + 7th

2. Preparation by a previous chord having note 4.

II   V⁷   IV   V⁷   II⁶   V⁷   IV⁶   V⁷

Handel: *Water Music*

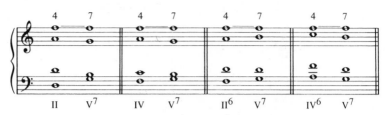

II⁶   II   II⁶   V⁷

3. Movement by leap.

Bach: Prelude in A from *The Well-Tempered Clavier*, Book I

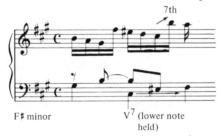

F♯ minor   V⁷ (lower note held)

When one voice leaps to the 7th another voice usually stays on the lower note of the interval.

Part-writing problems

1. When V⁷ moves to I in four-part writing, the 5th of one of the chords is left out. In (a) the 5th is left out of I and the root is trebled. In (b) the 5th is left out of V⁷.

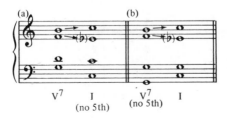

V⁷   I (no 5th)   V⁷ (no 5th)   I

This avoids awkward part-writing such as parallel 5ths, which may occur if both chords are complete.

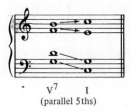

$$V^7 \qquad I$$
(parallel 5ths)

2. It is possible to use all the notes of each chord if the soprano moves 2–1 and the leading note (3rd of V⁷) falls to 5.

Bach: Chorale *Ich ruf' zu dir*

3. When V⁷ moves to VI both chords are often complete.

Bach: Chorale *Lob sei dem allmächtigen Gott*

$$V^7 \qquad VI$$
(complete)

$$IV \qquad I \qquad V^7 \qquad VI$$
(complete)

4. The 3rd or 7th may hide or disappear in an ornate version of V⁷–I, but it resolves when the harmony changes to I.

Mozart: Piano Sonata in C minor, K457

$$V^7 \qquad I$$

5. The 3rd and 7th of the chord may change voices before moving to I.

Beethoven: Solemn March from *The Ruins of Athens*

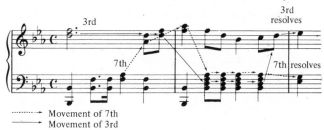

┈┈┈► Movement of 7th
───► Movement of 3rd

Inversions of V⁷

V⁷ has four different notes, so three inversions are possible.

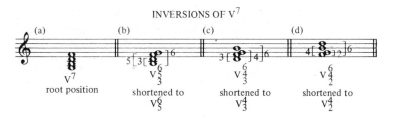

V⁷ inversions are prepared in the same way as V⁷. They usually move to I or I⁶, with the 3rd of the chord rising and the 7th falling.

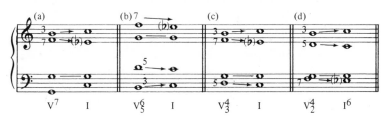

Haydn: 'The Heavens are Telling' from *The Creation*

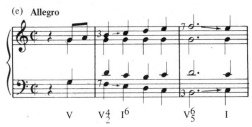

V⁷ inversions hardly ever move to VI.

Note that in V⁷ inversions:
1. The root of V⁷ remains in the same part when moving to I or I⁶; this is a common note to both chords.
2. The 5th moves to the tonic.

Uses of V⁷ inversions

1. To help move the harmony forward.

Beethoven: Piano Sonata in G, Op. 14 no. 2

F major V_2^4 I^6 V_3^4 I

2. To make rich harmony.

Beethoven: Piano Sonata in A flat, Op. 26

Maestoso andante

Ab minor V_2^4 I^6 I V_5^6 I   V

3. To make a smoother bass line.

Bach: *Brandenburg Concerto* no. 1 in F

Bb major V^6 V_5^6 I VII^6 V_2^4 I^6 VII^6 VII I^6 V^6

* = Accented passing note

4. V_3^4 as a passing chord.

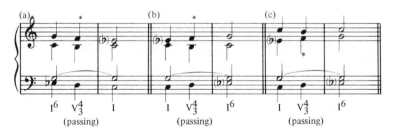

(a)   (b)   (c)

I^6 V_3^4 I   I V_3^4 I^6 I V_3^4 I^6

(passing)   (passing)   (passing)

Mozart: Piano Sonata in A, K331

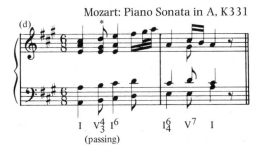

I   V$^4_3$ I^6 I$^6_4$ V^7 I
(passing)

(In (b), (c) and (d), note the unusual movement of the 7th, rising with the bass line.)

5. V$^6_5$ as an auxiliary chord.

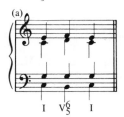

I   V$^6_5$ I

Mozart: *The Musical Joke*, K522

I _____   V$^6_5$ _____   I _____

6. V$^6_5$ as a bass arpeggio or broken chord.

Mozart: Piano Sonata in B flat, K333

C minor   V$^6_5$

WORK ON THE DOMINANT 7TH

1. Write V⁷ or one of its inversions before each of these chords so that the parts resolve correctly.

Example:

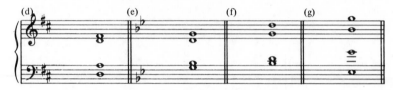

2. Resolve these V⁷ chords correctly.

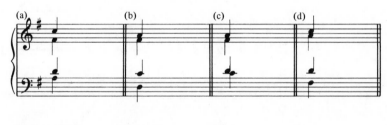

3. Insert a suitable V⁷ or inversion where marked.

4. Prepare and resolve these V⁷ inversions.

Example:

Preparation V⁶₅ Resolution

5. Write the following progressions:
a) I⁶₄ V⁷ I in B flat major
b) I V⁷ VI in D major
c) V⁴₂ I⁶ V⁴₃ I in C major
d) I⁶ V⁴₃ I in G minor
e) I V⁴₃ I⁶ in C minor
f) I V⁶₅ I in E major
g) I V⁴₂ I⁶ in G major.

6. Harmonise these fragments, each of which must contain at least one V⁷ or an inversion of it.

7. Harmonise these melodies using root positions, inversions and the dominant 7th where appropriate.

Hymn Tune: *Albano*

1.

Welsh Folk Song: *The Rising of the Lark*

2.

Irish Folk Song: *Golden Slumbers*

3.

Spiritual: *Go Down Moses*

4.

Musical analysis

There are four stages to go through when analysing a short piece of music. Let us look at Beethoven's *Ecossaise* no. 1 and use the plan on the following pages to discover more about the piece.

Beethoven: *Ecossaise* no. 1 (c.1823)

APN = Accented passing note
* = Climax note

Stage 1
FORM

1. Number of bars in the piece   *32*
2. Number of phrases   *4*
3. Number of bars in each phrase   *Phrase 1: 8 bars*
                                      Phrase 2: 8 bars
                                      Phrase 3: 8 bars
                                      Phrase 4: 8 bars

4. Are all phrases the same length?   *Yes. Each is 8 bars,*
                                      *   i.e. symmetrical*

5. Any other points of interest   *Phrases 1 and 2 are*
                                      *   identical except for a*
                                      *   modified ending*

Stage 2
PATTERNS IN
MELODY AND
RHYTHM

1. Does the melody consist mainly of
steps, leaps or a mixture of the two?   *Mainly leaps*
2. Is the range of the melody narrow,
medium or wide?   *Wide: 13 notes, C to*
                                         A flat

3. Which melodic shape is used, or is
there a mixture of different shapes?   *Phrase 1: wave + climax*
                                         Phrase 2: wave
                                         Phrase 3: arch
                                         Phrase 4: arch

4. How many motives are there? How
long is each?   *One motive, one bar long*
5. Are the motives melodic, rhythmic or a
mixture?   *Melodic and rhythmic*
6. Are there any characteristic intervals? *Leap of an octave in*
                                         *   Phrases 3 and 4*

7. Name the ways in which the motive(s)
is varied, e.g. sequence, inversion   *1. Approx. inversion*
                                         *   (e.g. bar 2)*
                                         2. Varied sequence
                                         *   (5–7)*
                                         3. Interval change
                                         *   (5 and 7)*
                                         4. Repeated exactly (6)
                                         5. Simplified (19 and
                                         *   21)*
                                         6. Varied and decorated
                                         *   (23)*

8. Where do the climaxes occur?   *Bars 8, 23 and 31*
9. Name the key of the piece   *E flat major*
10. Does it use major, melodic minor
(raised and/or lowered) or harmonic
minor?   *Major*

11. How are the motives used within the phrase?
(e.g. motive + variations, free material, two motives + variations, one motive for the whole piece)

Phrase 1: motive + variations
Phrases 2, 3, and 4 follow the same pattern

Stage 3
HARMONY

1. Analyse and mark each chord used

Mark in pencil on the music

2. Analyse and mark the bass root movements

Mark in pencil on the music

3. Are the bass root movements strong, medium or gentle?

Phrases 1, 2 and 4: strong
Phrase 3: mainly strong

4. Name the cadences at the end of each phrase

Phrase 1: imperfect
Phrase 2: imperfect
Phrase 3: perfect
Phrase 4: perfect

5. Name embellishing notes and list where they occur

Very few. There are accented passing notes in bars 2 and 4

6. Are there examples of passing or cadential $^6_4$ chords, auxiliary chords, etc.?

No

7. How many chords are used in each bar?

One chord in each bar, sometimes as a broken chord

8. Is this the same throughout the piece? If not, where does the harmonic rhythm change, and to what?

Same throughout

9. Outline the shape of the bass and compare this with the melodic shape

The bass line is almost stationary in Phrases 1 and 2. Phrases 3 and 4 are completely different. Here the bass moves strongly upwards by step in a broad sweep to reach the perfect cadences (23–24, 31–32)

10. Are there any key changes? Give details

No key change

Stage 4
SUMMARY OF
THE MAIN
POINTS OF
STYLE

You should now be able to write a summary of the main features and style of the piece using the information you have collected. Something along these lines would describe the general style.

In this short piece by Beethoven, harmony, melody and rhythm all help to make a perfectly balanced and symmetrical form. This quick and lively dance for piano is in simple duple time ($\frac{2}{4}$). It grows from a simple one-bar motive using a small interval range of only a 3rd. This short and cutting rhythm is heard continuously throughout the piece and develops into a wide-range melody. The repeated motive is at first rather static in its wave-like shape (phrases 1 and 2). This contrasts sharply with the fast rising pattern of phrases 3 and 4. The fast ascent and the strong, active bass root movements seem to push the music forward in a very energetic manner to the final perfect cadence.

WORK ON MUSICAL ANALYSIS

Write a detailed analysis and summary of the general style of these short pieces. Follow the plan step by step. Any points which you are not sure of should be checked in the appropriate chapter.

Hook: Gavotta from *Lesson* in C, Op. 81 no. 3

1.

Mendelssohn: *Sechs Kinderstücke*, Op. 72 no. 1

Purcell: Minuet from *The Second Part of Musick's Handmaid*